SMALL
COMFORTS

Also by Tom Bodett

AS FAR AS YOU CAN GO WITHOUT A PASSPORT
The View from the End of the Road

SMALL COMFORTS

❖

More Comments and Comic Pieces

❖

TOM BODETT

Addison-Wesley Publishing Company, Inc.

*Reading, Massachusetts Menlo Park, California New York
Don Mills, Ontario Wokingham, England Amsterdam Bonn Sydney
Singapore Tokyo Madrid San Juan*

Grateful acknowledgment is made to Harper & Row, Publishers, Inc., for permission to reprint two passages from the foreword to *Essays of E. B. White,* copyright © 1977 by E. B. White.

Library of Congress Cataloging-in-Publication Data

Bodett, Tom.
  Small comforts.

  I. Title.
AC8.B563 1987   .081   87-12804
ISBN 0-201-13417-9
ISBN 0-201-13689-9 (pbk.)

Cover illustration by Leslie Evans, from a sketch of the Bodett family hearth by Debi Bodett
Text design by Copenhaver Cumpston
Set in 11-point Galliard by Compset, Inc., Beverly, MA

BCDEFGHIJ-DO-898
Second Printing, November 1988
First paperback edition, June 1988

To Debi

My first editor, my best friend,
my lover, the mother of our child,
and, as luck would have it,
my wife

ACKNOWLEDGMENTS

I continue to thank Eileen Hughes and Joe Gallagher at KBBI, public radio for Homer, Alaska, for putting my stuff on the air in the first place. The folks at the Alaska Public Radio Network and National Public Radio's "All Things Considered" also deserve special credit for helping perpetuate much of the work on the following pages.

I'd like to thank Kathleen McCoy, my editor at the *Anchorage Daily News,* for letting me do whatever I wanted. Thanks also to Christopher Carduff and George Gibson, my editors at Addison-Wesley, for *not* letting me do whatever I wanted.

My wife, Debi, once again earns my undying love and gratitude for living with me through this project, and special thanks to my two-year-old son, Courtney, who, with time and a little luck, won't remember anything about it.

And last but never least, thanks to all my dear friends and cohorts around this little town who give me my ideas, keep me honest, and continue to let me believe I know what I'm talking about.

T.B., Homer, Alaska

CONTENTS

ix

INTRODUCTION

The essayist is a self-liberated man, sustained by the childish belief that everything he thinks about, everything that happens to him, is of general interest. He is a fellow who thoroughly enjoys his work, just as people who take bird walks enjoy theirs. Each new excursion of the essayist, each new "attempt," differs from the last and takes him into new country. This delights him. Only a person who is congenitally self-centered has the effrontery and the stamina to write essays.

I think some people find the essay the last resort of the egoist, a much too self-conscious and self-serving form for their taste; they feel that it is presumptuous of a writer to assume that his little excursions or his small observations will interest the reader. There is some justice in their complaint. I have always been aware that I am by nature self-absorbed and egoistical; to write of myself to the extent I have done indicates a too great attention to my own life, not enough to the lives of others.

It is always a great joy for me to stumble across insights and admissions by other writers, like those above by E. B. White, which spark instant identification. It's especially comforting to find certain familiar emotions and experiences expressed across time and social barriers with perfect authenticity. We've all had our moments when reading, at the theater, or listening to a gifted storyteller when we've stopped to say to ourselves, "Yeah, it's just like that." Such moments serve, for a time, to take a bit of the loneliness out of being human. This sharing of experience seems to me the only real purpose to produce or consume art of any kind.

Not having been trained as either an artist or a writer, I am all too aware of the audacity involved in presenting this collection of my thoughts on the world at large. I am not well educated or even particularly experienced in the wider scope of things. I've yet to commit an idea to paper that I didn't read later and think, "Who really cares?" I'm always pleasantly surprised when anyone does. It helps keep me going despite my lack of credentials.

By far the most striking characteristic of the life I write about is its bone-chilling normalcy. I'm a generic American. Reading a list of national averages is like leafing through my résumé. I'm of medium height and build, was raised in the Midwest, and assume more and more middle-of-the-road views as I approach midlife. I have one of those faces that remind people of a brother or old roommate. I take some satisfaction from all this, but am also painfully aware of being ordinary. We ordinary people lead ordinary lives full of ordinary things while we peer through windshields and TV screens at interesting surroundings. We're in the middle of the curve and haul around our 2.6 children in our

1.8 cars doing the best we can on average incomes. It's not a bad life. It is simply life as we know it.

We seem to spend a lot of time hungering after the details of the lives of the rich and famous, the up and coming, and just about everyone else we view as exceptional people. Most of us know more about Elizabeth Taylor than we do about our next-door neighbors. We celebrate our eccentrics at the expense of ourselves. This has always rubbed me a little in the wrong direction. I'm of the mind that there are no exceptional people. There are only normal people who sometimes do exceptional things.

Most of the exceptional things we do never hit the papers. Every once in a while we'll read of the local hero who drags the neighbors' kids from a burning building, or the poverty-stricken old widow who turns in the bag of cash she found on the street. These certainly are exceptional deeds and worthy of attention, but few of us will have the opportunity to imitate them.

The less newsworthy but every bit as exceptional things we do, we do in private. Quitting cigarettes is one of the toughest roads a person can ever travel. Letting your baby girl out the door on her first date is probably one of the most painful and selfless acts on record. Saving a failing marriage with patience and love deserves no less than the highest honors. There should be a Hall of Fame for these sorts of things.

There is also a flip side to all of this, one we're all too familiar with. Even though we mostly want to, and frequently intend to, we don't always do the right thing. The good intentions of ordinary people are constantly at odds with the world around them. We have our selfish desires, and our unreasonable fears. We make mistakes and are forced to look back on lives fraught with stupid remarks, cruel gestures, and sad regrets. We live with this guilt, and that is the price of being human. This, too, is life as we know it.

My only expertise in these matters is being a card-carrying member of this life as we know it. I don't expect that you out there will learn much from what you read in here. In fact, you'll probably come away reminded of an old friend or roommate. But that's all I really ask out of this deal. That and if at least once during the reading you stop to think, "Yeah, it's just like that."

I'm always comforted when a writer does that for me. I've tried to pay a little of it back with this collection, and hope you'll find some of that same sort of comfort on your way through.

TAKING POTLUCK

❖

Mood Piece

I had kind of a mood on lately. It lasted nearly a week before I snapped out of it. I was absolutely miserable and so was everyone around me. Bad moods are strange things. They seem to compound themselves and look for dark events to add to the gloom. Mysteriously, they can even cause them to happen. Some religions call this karma, others a loss of grace, but whatever it is, it stinks.

The bad mood scenario goes typically like this.

You wake up late, bound out of bed, and jam your foot under the closet door. This dislodges the big toenail from its setting, which hurts worse than if you'd taken the whole leg off at the knee. Recovering through rapid breathing, you throw on some clothes and fire up the coffeepot. While urging the brew cycle to its conclusion you sift through a stack of yesterday's mail and find a piece you'd overlooked, an official envelope from the City. It's one of those "Hold firmly here, grasp and snap" deals that never work. You put your fingers at the indicated points and give it a stiff pull, neatly tearing the entire packet in two. It turns out to have been your personal property tax statement, and the rip went precisely through the amount due, rendering it unreadable.

Your temples start to throb, so you pour a fresh cup of coffee and turn on the radio to try and settle down. A little music usually soothes, but instead of music you're met with a barrage of incomprehensible jazz being forced through a saxophone at a pressure of ninety pounds per square inch. It's about as soothing as listening to an aircraft engine seize up in a small room, so you snap off the radio with a finality that sends the volume knob rolling under the stove. You figure it's time to stop screwing around and go to work.

There is just the tiniest ball of rust bouncing around in your fuel filter. It's remained there harmlessly for months, biding its time for a morning such as this. Halfway to town, which is exactly as far as you can get from both home and a qualified mechanic at the same time, this little ball of rust decides to head north and lodge itself inside the opening of the main fuel jet. This shuts the engine off quicker than if you'd used the key, leaving you with absolutely no clue as to what went wrong.

After forty-five minutes of dinking around with a stripped-out crescent wrench, you throw up your hands and decide to thumb a ride to town for help. As you slam the hood shut on your shirttail, you think you hear the unmistakable snicker of a rust ball buried deep within the bowels of a disabled wonder of modern engineering.

Your gray mood has turned a deep charcoal, and walking into an auto repair shop is never a good way to cheer up. There's always some grim mechanic who's the hottest thing since the magnetic screwdriver and thinks you're the worst thing that could ever happen to an internal combustion engine, rust notwithstanding. No matter what the problem turns out to be, it's always something you did wrong, and he'll inconvenience his entire day to get you back on the road out of the goodness of his heart and a nominal fee plus tax.

As far as bad moods go, this one is getting downright dangerous, so you head back home to start over. Pulling into the driveway you accidentally flatten the sleeping cat that you never liked anyway, and feel just awful about it. When your wife sees the mood you're in, she thinks you did it on purpose, and you wonder why you didn't do it a long time ago if you're going to get blamed for it anyway. It starts to look like this string of bad luck is just never going to quit.

I saw a logger I once worked with get so mad about something he tore his clothes off, sat down in them, and cried. He looked so silly that everybody laughed, which made him so much madder he started throwing dirt and rocks at us. We laughed even harder at that and were doubled over with cramps and tears by the time he caught on and started laughing himself. We laughed ourselves out, he put his clothes back on, and we went back to work. After that, anytime a guy got really upset about something, he'd pretend to be tearing his clothes off, and everybody'd laugh. That would be the end of it.

I lost my ability to blow it off somewhere along the line, and have to make myself remember those logging days when ill-fortune settles in for one of its marathon visits. They say all humor is rooted in tragedy and it's our capacity to laugh that sustains us. Humans are the only critters who have this ability, and it's a good thing we do. It wouldn't look very good for the tourists if we all had to rip our clothes to pieces every time the truck broke down.

Mechanical
Inclinations

Machinery and I have an understanding: we hate each other. I just have a hard time when it comes to fixing things. This, along with my inability to spit very far, is the most disappointing aspect of my life as a man. I do have some mechanical inclination. It's an attribute of my gender. There's a certain amount of knowledge about things mechanical that is passed on genetically from man to boy. Even my little son, when presented with a toy tractor, knew that blowing air through his flapping lips is what a tractor sounds like. He'd never seen a tractor until that day, but innately knew as much about them as I do. When tractors don't sound like flapping lips, they're broken. Of course, knowing when something is broken and knowing how to fix it are two separate fruits altogether.

It is something of a tribal custom among the males of our species to hold forth on what we know about twirly things with gears and springs. If you want to entertain the menfolk on a slow Sunday, throw a broken lawnmower at their feet.

"Must be the spark. She ain't gettin' no spark."

"No, it ain't got fuel. Look, the plug's bone-dry."

"Gotta be a stuck valve, you can feel there's no compression."

"No spark, no fuel, no compression. That 'bout covers it. What do ya figure, Bubba?"

"This is one broke lawnmower."

If the afternoon progresses according to custom, the guys will completely disassemble the thing, find nothing wrong, put it back together, and it'll run like a top. They won't have the foggiest notion what they did to fix it, but they'll all take the credit.

"Musta been that hunk of dirt grounding out the magneto."

"No, was a piece of grit in the carburetor fell out when Bubba dropped it."

"All the bangin' around unstuck the valve. That's all it was, I tell ya."

I'm always the guy that runs for more beer.

My first inclination when faced with a piece of broken equipment is to pick it up and shake it. It works well on toasters, waffle irons, and sometimes lawnmowers, but it's a stupid thing to try with a pickup truck.

With a broken car or truck it's best to open up the hood, remove the air cleaner, shrug your shoulders in bewilderment, and try turning 'er over again. She'll start more often than not, and this supports my theory that most of the time machines break down they're only looking for attention.

I had the privilege and the horror some years ago of owning a small crane. I say "small" because there are bigger cranes, but I still had to climb a ladder to get into the thing. The reason I bring this up is that among all the devices on this earth craving attention, heavy equipment is by far the most starved for it. The general rule with large, dangerous machines is that you work *on* them just about as much as you work *with* them.

For this reason I owe what little I've learned about mechanics to that crane. I used it to drive pilings in Petersburg. My pile driver at the time consisted of a 1,200-pound weight I would pick twenty feet in the air then drop on a piling. As scientific as this sounds, you'd be surprised how hard it was on the equipment. What it finally came down to was this: I'd drive a piling, bolt everything back together, drive a piling, and so on.

It's when things actually did break that I ran into trouble. It so happens this crane was built in 1945 by a company that's been bankrupt since before the Korean War. I'd rather look for a hot date in a convent than try to find a replacement part for that thing. This led to what we'll call "creative mechanics," more commonly known as jury-rigging, and my only formal goodwrench schooling to date.

I'd won the Rube Goldberg award for improvisational tinkering three years in a row by the time I handed that sorry mess of cable and gears over to some other poor soul. My driving lesson to the new owner went something like this:

"That wire hanging out of the dash is your air brake 'cause the pedal linkage broke. It works good, but don't pull too hard. It's only a wire, ya know. If you want second gear, put it in third and then wind 'er out. Double-clutch and go back to second for fourth. She don't have third gear anymore, but don't worry, I got all the pieces out of the transmission. On the swing knob here, left is right and right is left, and don't try to boom down until you shove this block of wood up under the hoist. I guess that's about it. If the engine catches fire, just jump outa there and hang back for a while. It usually goes out all on its own."

I've never really wondered what became of that crane. I only worry what's become of me because of it. I'm pretty careful about most of the things I do. My woodwork fits, my pants fit, and I habitually look up words I don't know how to spell. It's only machines that bring out the hack in me. If the glove compartment latch quits working, my solution is to wedge a folded-up matchbook in the crack. I spray WD-40 like it was bug spray at funny noises wherever they occur. If that doesn't fix them, I get used to the noise.

My tool box contains two hammers (one large, one small), a pliers, and three different gauges of baling wire. This is the combat gear I employ against all my broken gadgets. Come dangling muffler, flapping fender, or dead snow blower, there's nothing that a couple hammers and a little wire won't fix.

It's not something I'm terribly proud of. I win my little battles but ultimately lose the war. My mechanically inclined friends shake sorrowful heads at my contraptions, then shake them at me. I try not to take it personally, but this deficiency of mine does get on my nerves. Sometimes it makes me mad enough to spit — but not very darned far, I'm afraid.

Wood: You Can Count on It

I had an opportunity to become intimate with my wood-pile this morning thanks to our recent storm. If it's true what they say about comets being dirty snowballs of ice and rocks, then I had sort of a homemade Halley's laying in my front yard, with wood where the rocks should have been. First the wind blew the covers off the pile, then it injection-molded snow into every little nook and cranny of it. As woodpiles are well known for their nooks and crannies, I was faced with the engaging task of prying up each piece of wood, knocking the snow off it, and putting it down some-place else. I threw myself at this brainless endeavor with high abandon and let my mind lapse into a little woodpile reminiscence.

The pieces that were pretty small I knew must have been split early on the day I had the hydraulic splitter up here. As that day wore on and one cord led to another and another, the pieces of split wood grew decidedly bigger. By the fourth cord I was considering buying a wood-fired blast furnace and just leaving the logs in the round.

I remembered wondering the day I started the pile what happens if you lay your wood right on the ground instead of putting it up on pallets. As I beat it from the frozen earth with big hunks of turf stuck all over it, I decided it wasn't an experiment worth repeating.

I worked my way through the pile piece by piece. I admired some nicely shaped dry specimens, and snarled at others with knots protruding from them and wispy hairs of grain, evidence that a struggle was had on the wood splitter.

"Ah, wood," I thought, obviously drunk with the tedium. "What a wonderful way to stay warm." It's an *alive* heat. You can hear wood heat, but not like you hear an old furnace or the creak of an electric baseboard. It's an unpredictable noise. A pop in the night will sometimes wake you; you realize it's only the wood stove sounding off and curl back into the blankets, assured of your warmth. Heating with wood is finding a red-hot bed of coals in the morning and coming in from the porch shivering with a log in each hand. It's letting 'er roar for a while just to take the chill off while you contemplate the day ahead. It's also looking out the window at the neatly stacked pile of wood, knowing you've got a whole bunch of warm days out there all bought and paid for.

Nobody's going to send you a gas bill if you use it. There's no calculating kilowatt-hours every time you turn up the thermostat, no staying intentionally cool because you're too cheap to toast. It's one big pile of comfort without price or definition. We gauge our wood reserves in *cords,* a loose quantity at best, and think in terms of seasons instead of monthly billings. It's all very romantic and countryesque, and I'm behind it all the way. At least I was until I moved the woodpile.

I have this really stupid habit. I count things. I don't know how it started. It could be a genetic defect. I just find myself counting things when faced with any dull, repetitive task. I count cars when I drive on highways. I count plates and cups when I do dishes. Sometimes I count steps when I walk. It drives me crazy mostly, but I keep on counting and look at it as a way of pacing myself for lack of a better excuse.

So as I moved my woodpile, the least interesting thing I've done all year, there I was: " . . . three hundred and fifty-eight . . . three hundred and fifty-nine . . ." In the end I was faced with the reality of having one thousand one hundred and eighty-seven pieces of wood left. You wouldn't think that would bother a person. It sounds like a lot. But I also happen to count pieces of wood as I haul them up to the wood box every morning. Nineteen. Nineteen pieces of wood, more or less, every day.

What this means is I have exactly sixty-two and a half days of wood going for me. That means about two in the afternoon on February 7 I'm going to have a problem.

So much for the big pile of comfort without price or definition.

Every day, now, I'll count off nineteen pieces and brood as I take all that hard work, bring it up to the house, and set it on fire. I get a little crabby thinking about it. Now when I walk in the house with wood, I'll chuck it in the stove with ill-concealed spite: "Here ya go, have this one! Want another? Here! Here, take it all!" I'll slam down the lid. "Must think this stuff grows on trees!"

This afternoon I took a walk around the place and discovered the same storm that forced me to take inventory of my wood supply had also blown over about the nicest spruce on the lot. On any other day I'd have been a little heartbroken over this. I'd have kicked at the stump, shrugged my shoulders, and gone to tell my wife, "We lost the big one," like the dog just died.

But this didn't happen. I started to drool as I walked up and down its length: ". . . twenty-four . . . twenty-five . . . twenty-six. . ." My spirits were picking up for sure: ". . . forty-two . . . forty-three. . ."

The way I have it figured, I can get enough wood out of that spruce to take us through March if we burn the branches too, and by God, that tree next to it is looking a little sick itself. Probably fall down all on its own and leave a big mess. So let's see what we got here: ". . . sixty-eight . . . sixty nine. . ."

Old Friend
Guilt

There's something funny going on around here. I'm ready for winter. No kidding. All the firewood I'll need for this year and part of next is put away. The house is buttoned up and the snow tires are on the truck. I'm not bragging about it, I'm worried about it. This has never happened to me before, and I'm not so sure I can handle it. My winter income is secured, and there's little more I can do but chew on the lip of my coffee mug and watch that gloomy southwesterly pad through the hills like a big gray cat. Oh good God, *poetry,* I'm even writing poetry. What's going on here? That "fog comes on little cat feet" routine is for pampered poets of other places, not for me. I'm supposed to be out in a forty-knot driven rain trying to get a chainsaw started over a log that's going to be too wet to burn until June.

I should be outside inspecting window caulk, or up on the roof with frozen fingers gluing down wind-damaged shingles. But it's a new house. All that stuff's done. There's not another place for a bead of caulk anywhere on it. The skirting is tight, the pipes are insulated, even the truck's got enough antifreeze in it to make a polar expedition. It's driving me crazy.

My good ol' "I'm too busy to talk now" stride has fallen away to a "Wanna play some cribbage?" shuffle, and it's only October. That's not supposed to happen until February when we all run out of money and can't afford to move around a lot.

All my friends are too preoccupied with their own preparations to be of any use right now. I think maybe I should go help them with their wood and general battening down of the hatches, but then they'd be in the same boat I'm in. I'd just hate to do that to them. Hanging around, reading novels, writing letters, throwing darts. Gag me with a *TV Guide*. Give me thirty feet of heat tape and a damp crawl space any ol' day of the week.

I've never been a big one for self-motivation. It takes a certain amount of guilt in the air to get me to plant both feet next to the bed each morning. Last winter I was fortunate and had a half-finished addition stuck on the front of the house to worry about. Every day I'd get up intending to do something about it, but then it'd rain, or snow, or blow, or I'd run out of nails and have to give it up. Boy, those were the days. Each morning waking up to stare at the ceiling and say to myself, "Get going, you lazy slob. Your wife's pregnant, the house is cold, and nothing's going to get done if you don't do it." So I went and did it. Now I wake up to stare at the ceiling and stay that way.

Like many Alaskans, I think I'm mistaking contentment for boredom. Maybe it's because of the antagonistic relationship we keep with our weather. It's like an ongoing friendly argument that we miss when it's over. You say, "I think I'll patch the roof today," and the freezing rain says, "Oh no you won't." You think, "I'll just sit and read my paper this morning," then the wind comes through the front door and asks, "Why don't you fix this rotten threshold instead?" We come to rely on that after a while. We get trained not to count on anything. It's a spooky, lonesome feeling to say to yourself, "I'm going to watch Donahue, write for a couple hours, then take a nap," and have the elements agree, "Good idea." What do you do in a case like that?

I think I know what I'm going to do. I've got about a gallon of paint here that will get half of one side of the garage covered. If I start now, I'll run out of paint by dark, and by the time I get around to buying some more, it will be too cold to finish the job.

Every day I'll be able to look out the living room window at the half-painted wall. My wife will say, "I can't believe you started that and didn't finish." I'll shrug my shoulders in a familiar way, and smile at the return of my dear old sweet friend, Guilt.

Ditch Diving

The graceful winter sports of skiing, skating, and dog-sledding get a lot of attention around Alaska, but there's another winter activity that nobody seems to appreciate for the art that it actually is — ditch diving. We all become practitioners of this art at one time or another, but none of us seems to hold proper appreciation of what we're doing, perhaps because its aesthetics have never been fully defined for us. Allow me.

To dive you need a road, a ditch, some snow on the ground, and any licensed highway vehicle or its equivalent. Nothing else is required, but a good freezing rain will speed up the process.

The art of the dive is in the elegance with which you perform three distinct actions. The first one, of course, is that you and your car *leave the roadway*. Not so fast there, hotshot — remember, this is an art. The manner and theme of your dive are weighed heavily in this maneuver.

For instance, the "I wasn't looking and drove into the ditch" dive will gain you nothing with the critics. The "He wasn't looking and drove me into the ditch" dive is slightly better, but lacks character. The "It sucked me into the ditch" dive shows real imagination, and the "We spun around three times, hit the ditch going backwards, and thought we were all going to die" dive will earn you credits for sheer drama. The "I drove in the ditch rather than slide past the school bus" dive might win the humanitarian award, but only if you can explain to the police why you were going that fast in the first place.

Okay, so now you've left the road. Your second challenge is to *place the vehicle*. Any dumbbell can put a car in a ditch, but it takes an artist to put one there with panache. The overall appeal of your installation is gauged by how much the traffic slows down to gawk at it.

Nosed-in within ten degrees of level won't even turn a head. Burrowed into a snowbank with one door buried shut is better, and if you're actually caught in the act of climbing out a window, you're really getting somewhere. Letting your car sit overnight so the snowplows can bury it is a good way of gaining points with the morning commuter traffic. Any wheel left visibly off the ground is good for fifty points each, with a hundred-point bonus for all four. Caution: Only master-class ditch divers should endeavor to achieve this bonus positioning.

All right, there you are, nicely featured alongside your favorite roadway. The third part of your mission is to *ask for assistance*. Simply walking to a phone and calling a tow truck will prove you a piker and not an artist at all. Hit the showers, friend. The grace and creativity you display getting back on the road must at least equal those you employed while leaving it.

Let's say you were forced into the ditch and are neatly enshrined with one rear wheel off the ground and the hood buried in the berm. Wait until any truck bigger than your bathroom happens along and start walking in that direction with a pronounced limp. Look angry but not defeated, as if you'd walk all night to find the guy who ran you off the road. Look the driver in the eye like it would have been him if he'd been there sooner. This is a risky move, but it's been proven effective. If the truck has personalized license plates and lights mounted all over it, you're in good shape. Those guys love to show how hard their trucks can pull on things.

I prefer, however, to rely on the softer side of human nature. Addle-brained people hold a special place in our hearts, and I like to play on these protective instincts. If my car is buried beyond hope, I'll display my tongue in the corner of my mouth and begin frantically digging at the snow drift with my hands until someone stops to talk me out of it. If my hands get cold and still nobody's stopped, I'll crawl head-first into the hole I've dug and flail my legs around like I was thrown clear of the wreck. This works every time and has won me many a ditch-diving exhibition over the years.

I certainly hope I've enlarged your appreciation of this undervalued creative medium. I warn against exercising this art to excess, but when the opportunity arises, remember: Hit 'er hard, sink 'er deep, get 'er out, and please, dive carefully.

Sixty-Four-Dollar
Questions

Deep thinkers throughout the centuries have dedicated themselves to solving the great mysteries of life. Why are we here? What is death? How many angels can dance on the head of a pin? Who's in charge of all this? They've come out long on opinions, short on answers, and only served to muck things up worse than they already were. So I'd like to propose that these guys back off from the eternal questions for a while and put their heads together on some of the puzzles we face every day. Having solutions to even a few of these could go a long way toward quelling a lot of the fear and anxiety that make up our stay on this strange planet.

Take those little colored stickers that turn up on some of my mail, those fluorescent green and orange labels with the single letters on them, *C, D,* or *F.* Who puts them there? What do they mean? It makes me a little nervous to receive a letter and find that I'm an *F.* I don't like being classified in a system I know nothing about. Is this a contest I haven't heard of? Am I supposed to save them? If I get enough to spell out the name of the state I live in, do I win something? Put your mind to that, Plato. I want to know what's up here.

As long as we're on the subject of the postal service, who decides what goes on stamps, and why do we have seashells on ours? Have we run out of important people to commemorate and now have to use these mollusks to keep from issuing blank ones? The Canadians get Queen Elizabeth, and we get the frilled dogwinkle. What does this mean, and is it something I'm supposed to worry about?

After they've explained away those, I hope they'll have a go at this one: How do grocery shopping carts escape, and why do they end up where they do? More important, why aren't we surprised to see them there? When we find one in the middle of a field or overturned on an exit ramp, we never say, "What's that shopping cart doing way out here?" We just think "Oh, there's another one," and go on about our business. I swear if there'd been a shopping cart waiting at the foot of the ladder when Neil Armstrong climbed out of the *Eagle,* nobody would have paid any attention to it. We're so used to seeing them in strange places they've become invisible to us. What causes this? Could it have military applications?

And as long as we're in the mood, let's pose a few more questions. Why did they stop making the '64 Chevy pickup? There was nothing wrong with it. Where did all this oil come from? I thought we were supposed to be out. If they've stopped creating "Star Trek" episodes, how come I keep seeing new ones after watching it for fifteen years? Same goes for "M*A*S*H" and Ernest Hemingway novels. Can we look forward to any more Steinbeck in the near future?

Forget about the chicken and the egg, how far is up, and where does the time go. Just tell me where the lids to all my trash cans went, and can I find my missing socks there too?

Come on, all you poets and philosophers, preachers and professors. Earn your keep. These are simple riddles with undoubtedly simple solutions. People need to know these things. Take care of us on this and we'll let you get back to the eternal mysteries. And while you're at it, tell me this: Just what *is* the sixty-four-dollar question, and why does it cost so much?

Bad Signs

As one of the most modern and well-educated citizenries in the world, you'd think we could take pretty good care of ourselves, that we could drive cars, shop in stores, and heat up a can of beans without a lot of supervision. That doesn't seem to be the case. Every place you look we are warned about things that we shouldn't need to be warned about, and reminded of things that should go without saying. Either we've all gone soft in the head, or we were among some of God's dimmer creations in the first place.

It begins as soon as you get in the car. Bells and whistles go off, lights flash, and the simple matter of starting the engine takes on the feel of an emergency dive in an attack submarine. You sit back dumbly as a four-wheeled hunk of chrome and plastic orders you around. Fasten your seat belts! Close the door! Check my oil! And for god's sake put some gas in me!

After that bawling out, you drive to the store and are greeted by yet another command, PULL. But it's useless. We always push, then pull. Except on the way out, when we pull, then push. We don't need these signs on doors because we don't read them.

Once inside, you wander through the aisles and come upon a little stairway. STEP UP, it says. Oh, so *that's* how you work those things. You'd think a person who can show-er, shave, dress himself, and drive to town wouldn't need to be told how to operate stairs. Maybe STEP UP is a coy sales tactic urging you to buy something beyond your means and boost your social position.

Back home while putting up the groceries, you really get a talking-to. STORE IN WARM DRY PLACE. DO NOT FREEZE. DO NOT BOIL. OPEN CAN, PLACE PAN OVER OPEN FLAME OR HEAT SOURCE, SEASON TO TASTE. An old favorite of mine, DO NOT LITTER, has lately been re-placed. I have a bottle here I'm asked to DISPOSE OF THOUGHTFULLY. It's a kindly-worded phrase, but it doesn't make sense. I can meet the requirements of DISPOSE OF THOUGHTFULLY by heaving it in the river, then pausing to reflect on what a rotten thing that was to do. They should have stuck to DO NOT LITTER. It's less confusing.

Some commands are downright insulting. I was in a taxicab once that had a sign behind the driver's seat which read NO SPITTING, as if I looked like the kind of person that would spit in a taxi. People that would spit in a taxi probably couldn't read the sign, and would ignore it if they could. That sign should go.

NO SMOKING signs on self-serve gas pumps are the ultimate insult. Although there may be some individuals who don't understand the principles of octane, anyone who'd light up in a cloud of gas fumes would probably deserve everything he got. Mother Nature's cute little way of weeding out the bad apples.

Dumb signs like this are there only to protect the businesses that put them up. It's a sad commentary, but sooner or later some twit will blow himself up at a gas pump. A lawsuit will follow, with the family of the man begging the judge for sixty million dollars in pain-and-suffering compensation.

"Your Honor, he was a kind but simple man. He should have been warned that gasoline explodes." Case closed.

It occurs to me that if we all took more responsibility for ourselves, we could replace all these mindless instructions with reminders of real importance. DON'T WALK ON ICE WITH YOUR HANDS IN YOUR POCKETS. WRITE YOUR MOTHER. DON'T GO OUTSIDE WITH WET HAIR. Those are the sorts of things we do forget about.

But even those things, like all the others, could be covered with a single stern command. It's something my third-grade teacher used to use on me a lot.

"Mr. Bodett!" she'd snap.

"Yes, ma'am?"

"SHUT UP AND PAY ATTENTION!"

"Yes, ma'aaaam!"

Command
Performance

Up until a few days ago I was one of those people who didn't know a megabyte from an overbite, but that's all history now. I've joined the technocrats, that global group of future-minded individuals who embrace advanced technology and use it to their utmost advantage. I bought a personal computer.

Now, a personal computer is unlike all those other kinds in that, like a checking account or deodorant stick, you have it all to yourself. Other people can't just bop in and use it even if the spirit did move them to. This one is all mine, so keep your hands off while I run you through the details.

Like most new technology, computers can be a little scary to the uninitiated. The cavemen who first discovered fire no doubt circled around it cautiously, poking at it with sticks while daring each other to touch it. New computer owners do much the same with their machines. Once our cavemen finally did break down and touch the fire, they quickly got an idea of its basic properties. Technological advancement can be a very real and moving experience. Fortunately, most of the name-brand computers won't singe the hair off your knuckles. In fact, we don't even have hair on our knuckles anymore. You can see we've come a long way since fire was discovered.

Unlike fire, computers are what they call "user-friendly." Now, what I think that means is that those little boxes of microchips *like* you and want to hang around with you. Like dogs do. Just like our dogs, they are happiest when they're doing things for us. They want us to give them commands. So let's try a command here.

```
>SIT<
```

Let's see what it does with that.

```
<BAD COMMAND — TRY AGAIN>
```

You know, it's right. "Sit" is a bad command. It has domineering overtones and doesn't really suggest the friendship we're trying to develop here. Let's try this, then:

```
>PLEASE TAKE A SEAT<
```

That's better.

```
<BAD COMMAND — TRY AGAIN>
```

Oops. There it goes again. Obviously it either doesn't feel like sitting, knows it already is sitting, or considers it too elementary a command to deal with. Maybe it's looking for something a little more complex. Probably wants to impress me and win my undying friendship. Let me find a more advanced function. Here's a key that says SEARCH on it. Let's see what that does.

```
>SEARCH<
<SEARCH FOR WHAT?>
```

Now we're getting somewhere.

```
>NORTHWEST PASSAGE<
```

That should keep it busy. Oh good, it's making little noises. Must be working on it.

```
<NOT FOUND>
```

Not found? It sure couldn't have looked very hard. That's all right. I know where it is anyway, and it's a stupid route to take. Let's have it look around for something a little more practical and closer to home. I'll have it search for my lug-nut wrench. I haven't been able to find it all summer. Here goes nothing:

```
>LUG WRENCH<
<NOT FOUND>
```

There it is again. What good is this thing? How about this:

```
>SEARCH FOR YOUR PLASTIC BUTT WITH
BOTH HANDS<
```

```
<NOT FOUND>
```

I knew it. Either I've got a real lemon of a computer here, or an exceptionally lazy one. How about this MOVE key:

```
<MOVE WHAT?>
>MOVE YOU!<
```

That oughta burn its brain box.

```
<MOVE WHERE?>
```

Oh, how easily it fell into my trap. Let it flop this around its disk drive for a while:

```
>SEATTLE! HOUSTON! BACK TO SILICON
VALLEY! I DON'T CARE JUST GO!<
<BAD COMMAND — TRY AGAIN>
```

A mutiny, is it? I might not be able to move this over-rated high-tech stick-in-the-mud to do a darn thing for me, but I'll tell you one function I know how to use. It's this big red switch on the side of it that says OFF.

```
<  >
```

There, that worked.

So, as you can tell, these computers are nothing to be afraid of. Now you know as much about them as I do. If you have any questions, just give me a call. I'd be happy to walk you through this last procedure.

See and
Be Seen

E yeglasses have come a long way since that regrettable
day twenty years ago when I got my first pair. It didn't
seem that so many people wore glasses then. What a hor-
rible injustice to serve on a kid. There were two basic styles
to choose from, boys' and girls'. A boy got plain black
frames, big or small, thick or thin, depending on how big a
deal he wanted to make of it. A girl got plain, small,
thick black frames with little wings on them, to which
optional paste jewels might be added for style. As a boy,
wearing glasses put you into that class of kids who were
good at science but couldn't do very many chin-ups.
Since the nose doesn't develop until well into puberty,
elastic straps had to be worn to keep the frames on your
face. This gave your friends something to fiddle with in the
lunch line, and ultimately led to some customized repair
work with a variety of tape and wires. Things got a little
better later on.

John Lennon ushered in the era of wire-rimmed

frames, and many a young four-eye was able to recover any hipness he may have lost a few years earlier. But of course it was all for show, and private suffering endured behind those fashionable frames. Little did the sharp-sighted abstainers realize those wires constantly sawed away at the fleshy spot where the ears attach to the head and left huge pink pits on the sides of the nose where all the weight of the glasses bore down on two tiny spots. The nose pads left the tender young schnoz permanently furrowed, lending a whole new meaning to the term "groovy."

It's been blamed on everything from color television to self-abuse, but over the years more and more people began wearing glasses. The eyewear industry rose to the challenge of pleasing them all. Optometrists' walls are now lined with choices, and what's a modern shopping center without an eyeglass boutique? What once were purely functional gizmos to prop corrective lenses in front of our eyes are now nearly a fashion accessory. You can get the most delicate little wafers of glass set in gold designs as fine as any jewelry. There are sweeping multicolored plastic frames holding lenses the size of windshields. You can make statements with smiley faces, hearts, or butterflies etched into the extra glass, or have them tinted in a variety of ways to become a person of mystery.

The age of the eyesore eyeglass is dead. All the old black frames have been either made into safety goggles for machine shops or given to auto industry executives to wear in car commercials to make them look like on-the-job sorts of guys.

There are even those more plain of face among us who wear noncorrective lenses and use glasses only to enhance their features. Vanity aside, that is the craziest thing I ever heard of. I can't for the life of me think of a single reason to wear glasses other than to see things.

Although I'm sure they're not as bad as false teeth, crutches, or hearing aids, I think glasses fall into the same category of inconvenience. In the winter they fog up when you walk indoors. In the summer little bugs stroll around on them to appear as large dogs on the optic nerve, while sweat and gravity team up to slide them off the tip of your nose. Small children love to yank them from your face, taking tiny pieces of ear flesh along with them. When they get misplaced they are bound to turn up exactly where you decide to sit down and think about where you left them.

This is not the only time they become a pain in that general vicinity. After several months of wiping dust and fingerprints on shirtsleeves, restroom paper towels, and seat cushions, the subtlest little lines become etched in the lenses. These serve to provide you with a mind-bending light show every time you go to a movie or watch TV in the dark.

Contact lenses might offer a release from all of this, but not for me. I tried them once on a whim, and the act of installing them endeared itself to me as much as sticking poker chips under my eyelids would. The enemy could learn anything they wanted from me by making me wear contacts.

I guess I'll learn how to live with the foggy view, scarred nose bridge, and sore ears, but I won't have to like it. My secret fantasy (way before a Pulitzer, Cybill Shepherd, or Cybill Shepherd's sister if she has one) is to wake up one morning and see things clearly. You'd think that after twenty years of wearing glasses I'd be used to them and wouldn't think about it so much. Well, I just can't help it. Every place I look, there they are.

Taking
Potluck

Of all the wonderful distractions that summer has to offer, none is quite as wonderful as the potluck. I know it isn't strictly a summer event, but a potluck takes on much broader dimensions in the warmer months. It's held outdoors, usually accompanied by horseshoes or volleyball. The children run circles around each other, and the fish is fresh.

Fish is a staple of the Alaskan potluck, and I've never been to one that didn't have at least three species of it on hand in one form or another. Back in the Midwest where I first sat down to one, you could ruin a good potluck by bringing fish to it. People are suspicious of fish back there, and I'm sure the expression "smells fishy to me" originated at a community feed somewhere in northern Indiana. Fried chicken is the heart of the Great Plains foodfest, but outside the entrée, the ingredients of a good potluck are pretty universal.

Start with a large folding table on an uneven lawn and invite a bunch of people over. No matter what happens someone always brings too much fish, so there's no need to worry about the main course. Then wanders in a pot of beans and weenies and a relish tray with rolled-up cold cuts splayed around a radish-and-celery arrangement. Someone always brings marshmallows so the kids have something to get stuck in their hair, and a bachelor or two will show up with a six-pack and a bag of Doritos.

No fewer than five potato salads will appear in rapid succession. You have to like potato salad if you're going to like potlucks. In fact, I think the "pot" in "potluck" is an abbreviation for "potato salad", and the luck refers to those few fortunate individuals who can get through the meal and not wear some of it home.

Everything is served up on paper plates with the constitution of flour tortillas and eaten with little plastic forks that couldn't pry a bone from a cooked cod let alone penetrate your neighbor's lasagna.

Potlucks are hardest on those who do the cooking. They hover around the food table to see what's going over the best. "Now, no one has touched the three-bean salad. What's the matter with you people?" The builder of the salad turns the color of the red-cabbage clam dip and slinks toward the beer cooler. The hero of any potluck is the one who brings the deviled eggs. They are usually devoured before the other folks can even get the tin foil off their casseroles.

After one or two courses your plate has become something of a trough folded in the palm of one hand. An amazing blend of flavors is then inevitable. The juice from the fruit-and-nut salad seeps in under your uncle's world-famous beef-and-bean burritos, and the hot sauce from that makes an interesting topping for the fresh apple crumb cake you discovered while going back for one more bratwurst.

In a while most folks will have had their fill and will wander off sleepily in small groups to toss horseshoes or slap mosquitoes. There's always one or two guys who linger to graze at the table, but their picking has no real spirit behind it. A survey of the ravaged spread will reveal a half-dozen potato salads with one scoop out of each and a large basket of wholly untouched fruit.

I got an idea from this. You see, in this season of multiple potlucks it's not unusual to be invited to more than one on a single day. You can't make a different dish for each of them, so I recommend you make a potato salad and take the paprika shaker along with you. When you leave the first party, just smooth over your salad with a spoon and put some fresh paprika on top. No one will know the difference, and you'll be able to gracefully enter potluck after potluck.

To be prepared for the improbable — like if someone actually eats all your salad — keep a basket of plastic fruit in the car at all times. This will get you into the next party and it's perfectly safe, as no one ever eats the fruit. I glue them all together in case those lingering grazers get nosy and try to get them out of the basket. They usually give up after a few dispirited tugs and wander off to test the potato salads.

Of course, I don't recommend everyone follow my advice on this. *Somebody's* gotta bring the fish.

Off the Top
of My Head

There's something about a haircut that gets on the wrong side of me. I don't know quite what to make of it, but like most things, it can probably be traced back to an impressionable youth. Even in those innocent days when short hair was not only acceptable but stridently enforced, nothing was more humiliating than to show up somewhere sporting a new haircut. Girls would giggle and boys would mess it up with their hands while a blush worked its way into a freshly raised hairline. Of course, not all of this was without reason.

I used to get haircuts from my dad. When my brothers and I started to get a little shaggy — shaggy being defined as having hair that actually laid down on our heads — he'd line us up in the kitchen on a Saturday night. He had a haircutting kit made up of electric shears, a soft brush, and a scissors. I still don't know what the brush and scissors were for. He went at us with those shears in much the same way a rancher goes at sheep, except sheep don't put up near the fuss that we did. By the time he was done with us, we'd all be in tears and rubbing heads that felt like the passive side of a Velcro fastener. Well-worn Little League caps that were perfect fits just the day before now slid around uselessly, even though we'd fight within an inch of our lives to keep them on our scalps to hide the damage.

As we got older Dad gave in to our protests and let us have our way with a new hairstyle called the Pineapple. Now, the Pineapple was a haircut ridiculous enough to rival anything I've seen on the head of an eighties punker. It consisted mostly of no hair anywhere except right in front. A little knot was left on the forehead for no reason I can think of now other than to demonstrate what color your hair would be if given a chance to show itself. Of course we all looked like highway accident casualties, and my dad finally gave up on the shears altogether. Probably a kind word from a close friend like, "God-darn, Pete, those kids are ugly," helped to persuade him.

When left to grow our hair out to lengths we could actually pinch between our fingers, the first thing we did was smear it with grease. Brylcreem, Vitalis, Butchwax. We could've stayed afloat in heavy seas standing on our heads the whole time. Those were the days. Peel the pillow case off our hair in the morning and head right down to the bathroom mirror to try and make it look just like the guys on "Route 66."

Then the Beatles came along and screwed up everything. I think I was fashionable once for about twenty minutes when I was twelve, then it was off to the barber. They used to call them barbers. Now they're hair stylists, hair sculptors, and tonsorial artists. Back then they used to cut your hair and talk about the weather. Now they cut your hair and talk about hair. I think I liked it better the old way.

Except it wasn't any fun to be a kid in a barber shop. Barber shops were where men went to look at magazines and tell rancid jokes. They had to stop telling their jokes when I showed up, and all the really interesting magazines disappeared under their smocks. There were no redeeming qualities to a trip to the barber. Just when I thought I was a dead ringer for Paul McCartney, I'd be reduced to looking like a fourth-grader at a parochial school. Which wasn't too far from the truth, seeing as I was in the sixth grade at the time.

Still later it became fashionable to look like Jesus Christ with a bad attitude, and by then I was old enough to pursue the look, attitude and all. I let my hair grow in all its gnarled-up glory for many years. I resisted going to barbers to stay with the trend of the day, but now I go to hair stylists to resist the trend of the day. All the hairstyles I would have sold my sister for twenty years ago are once again the fashion, and I'd buy her back to keep away from them. The only magazines I find at the hair places are full of androgynous men with eye shadow, who get paid to look like Liza Minnelli. I won't get paid if I look like Liza Minnelli, and I refuse to do it.

I'm a big disappointment to my hair stylist, and it bothers me a little. I sound just like the old guys who used to hide their magazines from me at the barber shops. "Just take a little off the back and sides, and don't mess with my part." He always fluffs me up on the sly, but it's nothing that a hat won't fix.

Like I say, I never got along very well with haircuts, but I try not to dwell on it. I remember something else those old guys used to say. They'd see my little heart breaking as my hard-earned Beatle locks hit the floor and tell me, "You know what the difference is between a good haircut and a bad haircut?"

"What's that?" I'd moan.

"Two weeks, boy. Just two weeks."

Shake
<u>What</u> Thing?

O f all the peculiar things we find ourselves doing with each other in this world, dancing is the one that I've always had the most trouble with. It's not that I think it's immoral, nonproductive, or uncivilized. It's just that it's nigh on to impossible for me to do.

Oh, like most people I've done my little share of shuffling over the years. Back in my rutting days I'd appear on schedule every Saturday night at one hot spot or another to prey on available females. I'd compete with the other young bucks screaming their invitations over impossibly loud music. This most unnatural of rituals always made me feel ridiculous with no little help from my own natural awkwardness.

If the band played a tune I felt I could plausibly move to, I'd muster the courage to approach someone for a dance. Typically, as soon as I opened my mouth to shout my proposition, the band would abruptly stop. The room would become suddenly quiet except for my "WANNA DANCE?" hollered a half-second too late. My foiled prospect would giggle into her Tequila Sunrise as I returned to the perimeter to do my wall-paneling impersonation.

I'd hoped marriage would save me from all this humiliation, but I was sorely mistaken. Just because I don't go to the hot spots alone anymore doesn't get me off the hook. From time to time I still find myself in the unpleasant process of trying to dance.

I say "trying" because to this day I've yet to feel like I ever actually succeeded. I like music as much as the next person, but it doesn't seem to get very far past my eardrums. It just won't penetrate down into my bones and ligaments where it needs to be if you're going to dance with any kind of credibility. A really hot band on a really good night might find me making little squares out of cocktail straws while tapping one or occasionally both feet under the table. I'm having a perfectly fine time of it, but my partner is not impressed. She'll be led out to the dance floor by one or another handsome stranger until I can stand no more and plunge headlong into the fray.

This is where the real trouble starts. The only dance step I've perfected to date is jumping up and down and wagging my arms around. I lean over and ask my partner, "What do I do?," and she smiles, "Do what comes natural." I tell her, naturally, I'd like to go back to the table and finish my beer, and she says, "Don't be so self-conscious. Just do what everyone else is doing." So I look it over. I see someone swivel his hips; I swivel my hips. Some gal puts her arms up in the air; I put my arms up. If there's some shoulder jive goin' on, I try that. The overall effect is that I'm hung from the ceiling by my collarbone and being shook around like one of those cardboard Halloween skeletons. It's exhausting and embarrassing, and this bothers me.

I understand that dance is supposed to be celebration, a communal tribute to our love of life, each other, and our kinship with ancient rhythm. It's supposed to be expressive, revealing, even suggestive of inner desires. And there I am floppin' around like a cat on a clothesline. I don't like what this has to say about me and my link to ancestral harmony. The only thing ancient about my sense of rhythm is that it does get old after a while.

I boogie when I oughta woogie, rock where I oughta roll, and mambo all over a good tango. I don't know, maybe I just haven't found my niche yet. I've heard of this stuff called "square" dancing. I'll have to look into it. I hope it's something you do with cocktail straws.

Pet Peeves

It's been said that people who keep pets live longer. I hope that means they live longer than their pets. At least longer than *my* pets. It's a terrible thing to say and I'll probably end up in that circle of doggie hell where all the legless yap dogs go because of it, but I can't help it. I want to wring the necks of both my animals, and I don't know what to do about it.

I've had pets for as long as I can remember, but each of them found some way to die quietly before there were any serious rifts in our relationship. A string of hamsters, stunned birds, and chapped frogs worked in and out of a joyful childhood. Then of course there were the more durable breeds of the canine persuasion.

My folks kept wonderful dogs, the kind of exceptional animals that become part of the family. They could be spoken to in plain English, would fret dutifully when a kid was ill, and put up with all the degradations a houseful of sadistic children could engineer. They were never a problem and are still dearly missed.

Now I have a dog and cat of my very own, and I can't stand either one of them. I'm a little torn up about it. The cat, especially, has earned a certain amount of tenure around here — I've had him for ten years. He came into my life as a Christmas gift. (Oh. How nice. You shouldn't have.) I initially named him Shark Bait because that's what I had him figured as, but we soon became fast friends. I was a lonely young bachelor living in an unfamiliar Alaskan town, and having something soft and warm around the place was a real asset. His companionship was welcome, and he was a pretty good cat as far as cats go.

He'd do his business outside, was an accomplished hunter, and could swat the snot out of most dogs that messed with him. I guess what we had was a masculine bond. He tangled with a mink one time and got his face ripped off. I had to send him in an airplane to another town to have it fixed, and it cost me a hundred and fifty dollars. That says a lot about the way I used to feel about him.

After I married, he took to my wife more than me and turned into, well, a cat. Cream and egg yolks. He got bitchy and lazy, and I lost interest. I started thinking of him as a piece of furniture, and I guess I have for a long time now. At least until he started to lose control of himself. I've never had a piece of furniture make a mess like that before.

I'm sure it's just old age, but I can't forgive him for it. I mean he's not suffering. He sleeps in his own chair, goes outside when he's good and ready, comes in to eat dinner, then craps on the new rug. It wouldn't be so bad if he'd show some remorse, but instead he lies back in his chair with that "You should have known I was ready to go out" look on his face, the smug little face I once went to great effort to have re-secured to his skullcap. I just don't know what to do about it. I have a pest in my house. If he were a rat or a cockroach I would know what to do, but he's not. He's a pet. You can't exterminate pets, you have to murder them. I'm not a murderer.

The situation might not bother me so much if it wasn't compounded by the dog. I'm using the term "dog" pretty loosely. A wheelbarrow full of common garden vegetables would offer just as much companionship on a walk.

He's three years old and a beautiful specimen of a black Lab. All except for one thing. He was born with a head of solid bone. You could say he's a good-natured animal, but that's what they always say about stupid dogs. We have to keep him tied up all the time because he'll follow anything that moves. He's never been in much trouble with the neighbor's chickens or anything, but that's because the chickens can outsmart him. The trouble is that he's big and scary-looking, and nobody wants a big, scary-looking dog running around without a brain in its head. So he stays tied up, and we give him huge amounts of food for the pleasure of watching him lie in the sun and bark at clouds.

It's driving me crazy. When a terminal patient stops producing brain waves, he's declared legally dead. My dog's EEG is flatter than Kansas, but he's healthy as a horse and happy as a clam. We had him fixed a couple years back to see if he'd calm down and pay attention. All it did was calm him down. Now we have a cabbage on a chain in the front yard that eats its weight in Purina every month. Again, I don't know what to do about it. I harbored some hope for a while that he might redeem himself by eating the cat, but gave that up when I noticed the cat kicks him out of the doghouse whenever he feels like it.

I know I'm responsible for these animals. In fact, I can't stand people who mistreat or abandon their pets just because they've become an inconvenience. It's not their fault they drive me nuts, and it's not their fault they're mine. I can't do them in just because I screwed up. They might have been adopted by someone who likes stupid, lazy pets if I hadn't come along.

I could take them to the pound, but that'd just be letting someone else do the dirty work for me. I suppose if I tried hard enough I could find a benevolent soul to take them off my hands, but I can't bring myself to do it. It'd be like asking someone to take a beating for me. Even if they agreed, I'd feel lousy about it later.

What it boils down to is that I can only hope to outlive them. I look forward to maybe a handful of pet-free years before I take the big sleep myself, the sleep not even the bark of a one-hundred-pound dog could jerk me out of. I've buttered my bread and now I'll just have to eat it.

There's a lesson here someplace but I'm not sure what it is. I'll have to sort it out. I've heard of cats that live for twenty years or more, and as healthy as that dog looks, I'm going to have plenty of time to think about it.

Wait
Divisions

I read somewhere that we spend a full third of our lives waiting. I've also read where we spend a third of our lives sleeping, a third working, and a third at our leisure. Now either somebody's lying, or we're spending all our leisure time waiting to go to work or sleep. That can't be true or league softball and Winnebagos never would have caught on.

So where are we doing all of this waiting and what does it mean to an impatient society like ours? Could this unseen waiting be the source of all our problems? A shrinking economy? The staggering deficit? Declining mental health and moral apathy? Probably not, but let's take a look at some of the more classic "waits" anyway.

The very purest form of waiting is what we'll call the *Watched-Pot Wait*. This type of wait is without a doubt the most annoying of all. Take filling up the kitchen sink. There is absolutely nothing you can do while this is going on but keep both eyes glued to the sink until it's full. If you try to cram in some extracurricular activity, you're asking for it. So you stand there, your hands on the faucets, and wait. A temporary suspension of duties. During these waits it's common for your eyes to lapse out of focus. The brain disengages from the body and wanders around the imagination in search of distraction. It finds none and springs back into action only when the water runs over the edge of the counter and onto your socks.

The phrase "A watched pot never boils" comes of this experience. Pots don't care whether they are watched or not; the problem is that nobody has ever seen a pot actually come to a boil. While they are waiting, their brains turn off.

Other forms of the Watched-Pot Wait would include waiting for your drier to quit at the laundromat, waiting for your toast to pop out of the toaster, or waiting for a decent idea to come to mind at a typewriter. What they all have in common is that they render the waiter helpless and mindless.

A cousin to the Watched-Pot Wait is the *Forced Wait*. Not for the weak of will, this one requires a bit of discipline. The classic Forced Wait is starting your car in the winter and letting it slowly idle up to temperature before engaging the clutch. This is every bit as uninteresting as watching a pot, but with one big difference. You have a choice. There is nothing keeping you from racing to work behind a stone-cold engine save the thought of the early demise of several thousand dollars' worth of equipment you haven't paid for yet. Thoughts like that will help you get through a Forced Wait.

Properly preparing packaged soup mixes also requires a Forced Wait. Directions are very specific on these mixes. "Bring three cups water to boil, add mix, simmer three minutes, remove from heat, let stand five minutes." I have my doubts that anyone has ever actually done this. I'm fairly spineless when it comes to instant soups and usually just boil the bejeezus out of them until the noodles sink. Some things just aren't worth a Forced Wait.

All in all Forced Waiting requires a lot of a thing called *patience,* which is a virtue. Once we get into virtues I'm out of my element, and can't expound on the virtues of virtue, or even lie about them. So let's move on to some of the more far-reaching varieties of waiting.

The *Payday Wait* is certainly a leader in the long-term anticipation field. The problem with waits that last more than a few minutes is that you have to actually do other things in the meantime. Like go to work. By far the most aggravating feature of the Payday Wait is that even though you must keep functioning in the interludes, there is less and less you are able to do as the big day draws near. For some of us the last few days are best spent alone in a dark room for fear we'll accidentally do something that costs money. With the Payday Wait comes a certain amount of hope that we'll make it, and faith that everything will be all right once we do.

With the introduction of faith and hope, I've ushered in the most potent wait class of all, the *Lucky-Break Wait,* or the *Wait for One's Ship to Come In.* This type of wait is unusual in that it is for the most part voluntary. Unlike the Forced Wait, which is also voluntary, waiting for your lucky break does not necessarily mean that it will happen.

Turning one's life into a waiting game of these proportions requires gobs of the aforementioned faith and hope, and is strictly for the optimists among us. For these people life is the thing that happens to them while they're waiting for something to happen to them. On the surface it seems as ridiculous as following the directions on soup mixes, but the Lucky-Break Wait performs an outstanding service to those who take it upon themselves to do it. As long as one doesn't come to rely on it, wishing for a few good things to happen never hurt anybody.

In the end it is obvious that we certainly do spend a good deal of our time waiting. The person who said we do it a third of the time may have been going easy on us. It makes a guy wonder how anything at all gets done around here. But things do get done, people grow old, and time boils on whether you watch it or not.

The next time you're standing at the sink waiting for it to fill while cooking soup mix that you'll have to eat until payday or until a large bag of cash falls out of the sky, don't despair. You're probably just as busy as the next guy.

Cleanliness
vs. Godliness

The idea that cleanliness is next to godliness is a little presumptuous, don't you think? They've been telling us that all our lives, but I'm certain it's just a ploy to get us to pick up after ourselves. Who do they think invented dirt in the first place? How many of God's little critters would you let in on your living room rug?

I realize that hygiene is important to good health, but it's unnatural to be *too* clean. People who primp, pick, buff, and shine are spending way too much time thinking about themselves and their stuff and not enough about other things. The slobs of this world who blunder along whichever way it goes are in the true state of grace. Just compare the houses of the two.

The Cleanly has the kind you look at, the Godly's got the kind you live in. I was at one of those you look at the other day. I didn't have to take off my shoes at the door; I had to leave them at the end of the driveway. The glare in the kitchen was blinding, but I caught enough of a glimpse of the counters to see they were better organized than most surgical facilities. We didn't go in the living room, but my hostess let me stand in the doorway and admire things.

I remember touring the Robert E. Lee mansion as a kid and feeling like this. Little red velvet ropes cross the doorways to the rooms. You can look in, but not touch, and it compels you to speak in reverent tones. So I oohed and aahed reverently as I peered in at the rug and furniture.

The rug looked nice. It was freshly tended with a shag rake, she told me. I can't tell you much about the sofa or chairs. They were covered with that clear plastic sheeting. You know the kind: It has those little nodules on it to make sure nobody sits on it for very long. She had a big white cat on one chair and even it looked groomed, like it had a permanent, or had been dipped in solution to keep its hair from falling out all over the place.

The magazines on the coffee table were laid out in a fan shape next to a cut-glass ashtray. It glimmered with a rainbow warning to anyone who even thought of putting a cigarette near it. I couldn't see much else, as they had the curtains closed. "Fades the rug," she said. "Very nice," I told her, starting to feel like bird crap on an El Dorado.

We had coffee in the dining room. I could see the bottom of my cup clear through the coffee. A close inspection proved there was no little oil slick floating on the surface of the stuff. I was just getting ready to ask my hostess how she accomplished that when the handle of the slippery little teacup dodged from between my fingers. It broke on the iridescent tile, splashing a rather dark stain on her otherwise well-arranged white cat. It screamed into the living room in an impressive holy terror and climbed the curtains in a fabric-shredding frenzy. I never discovered the secret of her coffee, as she was soon showing me to the door and begging me to come again when I couldn't stay so long.

Sulking away like I'd just wet my pants in church, I decided to seek consolation at another friend's house on the way home. Now, this friend's got one of the other kind of houses: the kind you live in. And he's really very good at it. At his place you leave your shoes on to save your socks. "Wanna beer?" he called on my way in. "Sure," I said. "So grab one, and crack one for me too as long as you're up."

Here was a house my hostess would as soon set on fire as walk into, but I was feeling warm and welcome. I shoved some clothes, magazines, and what I think was *his* cat off an old easy chair and propped my feet up on the coffee table. We had a pitching contest with some old pistachio nut shells he had in a bowl. We flung them as close to the ashcan next to the wood stove as we could until they were all gone. He won.

He remained a perfect host by not telling me to keep my hands off things as I rummaged through a pile of old *National Geographics*. And he apologized graciously when I sat back on his sofa and found a handsaw I'd lent him a few months back. We made coffee, good coffee, strong enough that I couldn't see through the jar he offered it in, coffee with that tasty little Colombian grease slick on top. We played a couple of spirited games of living-room broom hockey with a piece of leftover breakfast toast, and I left for home feeling well visited and refreshed.

Yes, this cleanliness and godliness business just doesn't hold any water. I really don't think I'll have to wipe my feet before going through the Pearly Gates, or that Saint Peter will pick lint off my robes as he checks me out against the Big Book. I think instead he'll hand me a bag of pistachio nuts and direct me to a well-worn easy chair. At least I hope so. If I have to sit on plastic seat covers or endure the whine of a celestial Dustbuster, that eternal life they talk about is going to be way too long for me.

Strangers
in My Chairs

Furniture just seems to happen to us. There aren't too many people who get the opportunity to go out and buy a houseful of perfectly coordinated furnishings in one swoop. Royalty with summer homes or rock stars on sabbatical might enjoy the privilege at one time or another, but we mere mortals must go about things differently.

Our ideas about furniture, of course, started at home. For the most part, all the chairs and tables there were too big for any practical use other than making forts out of on rainy days. We were all made to sit straight at the table with our little legs dangling and our chins at plate level. There wasn't a piece of furniture in my folks' house that endeared itself to me in any way. Dad's chair was always fought over among us kids when Dad wasn't in it, but this was due more to its importance than its comfort. It was like sitting in the throne while the king was out of the castle.

Those of us who went on to college got little in the way of furniture education. The standard dorm fare — bunk

bed, desk chair, and lounge seat that sat like a straitjacket —
were enough to quell any notions of posture we might have
brought from home with us. Blaze orange burlap on blond
maple was the general theme, and an apple crate, a couple
of bricks, and a two-by-six were all the personal touches
required to finish off a room. The few stabs we made at
decorating were a festoon of fish netting and an Easy Rider
poster over the bed.

After college came our first real digs, furnished apartments, the term "furnished" being applied loosely. A hide-
a-bed made up of right angles and foam rubber sat beside a
three-legged overstuffed chair that was meant to have four.
Paperback westerns and sociology textbooks made up the
difference. The chairs in these apartments were hideous
misrepresentations of a place to sit. I remember my room-
mates and me complaining for weeks about a foul smell
around one such apartment before one of us discovered the
chair had been on fire. The smoldering mess of stuffing and
lint had spontaneously combusted, no doubt.

Our beds were stained mattresses on bare floors, and
the bricks and boards saved from college rounded out our
suites. Kitchen tables were of the tubular persuasion with
bright red simulated marble tops ringed with cigarette
burns. One advantage to this type of furniture arrangement
was that the place looked little better after we'd clean it up,
so there was no logical reason to even bother.

It seems that only after marriage do people take any
serious notice of furniture. After all, you can't set a shiny
toaster oven, matching cutlery, or a new bedspread on any
old thing. The early years are the hardest because you're
pretty much stuck with what you can afford. This usually
amounts to a coffee table of pressboard and photographic

wood-grain paper. This mode of furnishing is a by-product of the mobile-home industry. If you set a perfectly healthy plant on such a piece it would immediately turn to plastic.

Other appointments to the parlor setting might be two blow-molded end tables and a genuine imitation Old English vinyl recliner. Geologists centuries from now will excavate these artifacts and dub this the Plasticene Era. Some couples never snap out of this mode, and they may be the smart ones. Love comes and love goes, but plastic is forever.

Many among us, if left in one place long enough, will eventually settle on a motif. *Modern* might bring with it deep shags, La-Z-Boys with fabric on them strikingly similar to that which we left at our dorms, and an airbrushed bullfight hanging on the wall for a touch of class. *Traditional* is the same as Modern, only family portraits are on the wall in place of the bullfight. *Ultramodern* gets us back to metal tubes with a lot of glass and hanging things. Wall decoration might be jagged tin sculptures accented by a stripe running from the front door to the fern.

And still others will swing the opposite way and choose *Antique,* the used look. Acquiring this type of furnishing involves going to a lot of auctions run by people who gave up the carnival circuit to sell furniture. "Dis here buffet was made when King Louie da Fourteen still had all his hair, har har." We proceed to outbid each other for a rickety old dresser with stuck drawers and a blurry mirror.

I have a lot of this Antique stuff in my house, and I like it. Coming home is like going to Grandma's house everyday. A sense of permanence stays in the room with you. I stare at our hutch and wonder sometimes what treasures were stored there by people dead and gone who will never see our treasures so nicely displayed in it. I look at our hodgepodge of aging chairs and think of the strangers who may have taken a load off their feet in them. It's not necessarily beautiful furniture. Some of it is pretty plain. It's just interesting because it has longevity. Built-in memories.

Like a lot of us, I have a favorite chair. It's not very comfortable to sit in, and it's pretty beat-up to boot. It's a teetery old bowback I got some years ago. What's special about it is some carving on the bow. In crude letters gouged out by an unknown forebear reads, "I Love you M.K." I've never stopped wondering about that. Who carved it? Who's M.K.? Did they ever get together? Have children, grandchildren?

When I sit down to breakfast it creaks and croaks its "good morning" to the world. I'm reminded of that simple phrase behind my back and wonder about it all over again.

Now *that's* a piece of furniture.

Symptoms of Fatherhood

I used to swear I'd never be one of those guys who talk about their kids. (Of course, before that I swore I'd never be one of those guys who even *have* kids. So you can see how I am about swearing.) I've found, however, that something happens to a man when his own child is born, something rich and inexplicable and, so the experts tell me, chemical.

There has always been lots of talk about the hormonal imbalances and emotional trauma a mother experiences before and immediately after the birth of a child, but lately attention is turning to the effects of childbirth on the male glandular system. It's really quite astounding once you examine it. For instance, it's been proven that the male brain secretes an enzyme into the optic nerve shortly after the onset of fatherhood that allows a man for the first time in his life to see things in store windows like colored blocks and "Li'l Slugger" baseball jammies. It also enables him to tell a cloth diaper from a dipstick rag and a stuffed teddy from a mounted duck.

Another brain fluid, probably a mild sedative, is let loose in the hearing canal. Upon reaching the inner ear, this solution makes a man's head spin when he receives a smile or coo from his own loin fruit. More important, it also serves as a flap-damper against children screeching in public places or infants whining on airplanes. Sounds that once would make a man's fillings ache or compel him to tear an airline magazine in two now only leave him to stare dumbly at their source with an appreciative smile.

An ambivalent chemical, this same stuff that serves to dampen the sounds of everyone else's children can also actually attune a man's ear to those of his own. His hearing can become so sensitive that he'll bolt upright from a dead sleep should his child so much as gurgle in its crib downstairs through two closed doors.

Another biochemical, probably from a gastric gland, enters into a father's abdominal cavity in the postnatal period. This natural body fluid, technically known as *Papa-Bismol,* is, of course, a stomach relaxer. Foul and foreign substances, such as those to be found in a child's diapers, no longer trigger his gag reflex. It may even allow for closer inspections of them in times of illness or moments of simple paternal curiosity. Other infant malfunctions such as oral ejections (spit-up) or nasal discharges (snot) can be greeted with equal reserve under the influence of Papa-Bismol.

Quite frankly, some effects of childbirth on the male of our species are of totally unknown origin. One of these affects his sense of time and direction. Time appears to move at an accelerated rate as the child matures, and all roads lead home. Neighborhood watering holes lose their appeal, and dads are uncannily on time for supper for the first time in their married careers. It's entirely possible that this disorientation in space and time is responsible for the quirks which appear in a new father's speaking habits.

Normally articulate and well-spoken young men can be found leaning into cradles and bassinets repeating a string of guttural incantations. The ability to interpret language is simultaneously impaired. It's not unusual to have a new father claiming to have heard the word "daddy" from a child who's only utterance to date was that of passing stomach gas.

This stage quickly passes and is replaced by another speech anomaly, the *Couplet Stutter*. This causes the male parent to double words which previously served him well solo. Some examples: "no-no," "yum-yum," "bye-bye." In cases where a word cannot be doubled up and still make sense, the Couplet Stutter gives way to the *Aiee Syndrome*. For instance, the sentence "Junior sees the dog-dog" is meaningless, but "Junior sees the doggie" makes perfect sense to everyone but the kid, who can't understand why Dad has to *Aiee* every noun in the dictionary when he points it out.

These very speech afflictions may be responsible for other, yet-to-be-explained new-father nuances. Men who could not have given a hoot how *Babar Gets to Candyland* in prenatal years can be found engrossed in that particular narrative long after the child has given up for the evening. The story of the Three Little Pigs can lead to mild depression in fathers who don't get a chance to huff and puff the doors down before the kid nods off.

Renewed interest in ogres, trolls, fairies, and pirates generally prefigures the disintegration of formal education.

This just might be what is behind such irrational social behavior as pulling out wallet-sized baby photos in airport lounges or suggesting a petting zoo as an interesting night on the town.

Overall, as you can see from this definitive study, the male is much more likely than previously thought to be adversely affected by biological changes due to childbirth. Of course none of these symptoms of fatherhood has arisen in yours truly, and the only reason I'm aware of them at all is that I'm a voracious reader and get all my information from books.

In fact I'm in the middle of one particularly riveting volume at the moment. It seems there were these three men, and this tub. In an interesting blend of careers there was a butcher, a baker, a . . . hold on a minute. I think I hear something downstairs in the baby's room.

Dadiholics Anonymous

I lived with the illusion for eighteen months that I could become a parent without getting all "parenty" about it. It's only recently I've been able to admit that I can't. My name is Tom, and I am a Dadiholic. That's right. I've found I can't control my parental behavior, and it's seeping into other areas of my life. I'm starting to get worried. It's not that I feel I've become a danger to myself or society. It's scary, that's all, and I think I might need help. Take the case of the no thankyou's.

Long ago my wife and I decided we would not batter our son with a lot of unqualified noes. There is a stage in children's development (roughly from six months to eighteen years) when it's necessary to discourage them from certain unsavory behavior. In order to soften the blow of this steady barrage of badgering, we chose to add to each "no" a polite "thank you" as a sort of verbal candy coating. We afford this courtesy to almost every other person we refuse, so why not our own child? Now when he pushes peas up his nose, it's "No thankyou." When he gouges out the cat's eyes, "No thankyou." When he melts plastic trucks on the wood stove, "No thankyou." It's easy enough to do and didn't take too long before it became a habit. That's just the problem — habitual use of anything can lead to addiction. Enter woe and despair.

I've found that it's become impossible for me to utter a simple "no" without following it with "thankyou." Whether it's a moon-eyed evangelist peddling salvation at my front door or someone at the bank inquiring if I'm waiting in line, my answer is the same, "No thankyou." So what's the big deal, you're probably asking yourself. What does it matter if I'm a little more polite than I need to be, even if it is a knee-jerk reaction?

I'll tell you why. It's this old truck I drive. It has about ninety degrees of play in the wheel, and though I can keep it between the lines with little effort, it's not always a pretty sight. One of these days a policeman is going to get behind me and feel obliged to investigate. The following scenario is what I live in fear of.

"Pretty fancy driving, mister. Have you been drinking?"

"No thankyou."

"Do you mind stepping out of your vehicle?"

"No thankyou."

"Can you recite the alphabet?"

"Yes please."

"Can you say it backwards?"

"No thankyou."

You can see how I could no-thankyou myself right into a pair of chrome bracelets and an unscheduled tour of the pokey. If I don't somehow regain control, there's no telling what kind of trouble it could lead to.

The other thing I've caught myself doing away from the house is "yaying." Yaying is letting loose with a jubilant "yay" while rapidly clapping your hands together. Common household variety praise, and nothing to be ashamed of. Kids love it and usually follow suit with quick little hands and a grin cute enough to ensure they will live comfortably under your roof for the rest of their lives. The general public, however, does not respond as enthusiastically to a grown man yaying.

I've been having nightmares where I'm sitting in a tavern watching the seventh game of the World Series with a bunch of the boys. "The boys" are all two hundred and fifty pounds without an ounce of fat on them. They enjoy scratching up the beer pitchers with the stubble on their chins and chewing the vinyl cushion from the edge of the bar when the favored team makes an error. In the midst of this I see myself jumping from my stool and involuntarily yaying. I haven't slept a wink in four days, and my night sweats are ruining the bed linen.

I've only decided to go public with this now because I sense there are other dads out there with these same troubles — good fathers, dedicated husbands, and regular guys the world over just coming to grips with their Dadiholism.

I think we should organize meetings. One night a week to get out of the house. We could arm-wrestle or something to break the ice, then get on with the regular business. This might include one member pushing a toy dump truck across the room while the rest of us helped each other resist making motor noises with our lips. Assembly guides to Tinkertoy sets could be ceremoniously burned while we punched shoulders and sang old sailing songs.

Personal fears and experiences, like those I've mentioned above, would be shared with the group. We could exchange phone numbers to be used in time of crisis. If, say, at a hockey game things got out of hand, you could make your way to a pay phone: "Roger, I'm really worried tonight. I've almost yayed three times already, and it's only the first period."

"Calm down, Ralph. Go back in there and throw the ice out of your Coke at somebody, then tear the cup apart with your teeth. You're going to be fine, buddy."

Yes, gentlemen, I think it's time we got together on this thing. Stop suppressing your anxieties and shout it from the roof tops, "I am a Dadiholic." We can help each other. If we don't at least try it, we'll never know, thankyou.

A Housebuilder's Guide
to Homemaking

Women have been complaining for years about being strapped with the household chores and the duties of child care with little appreciation, less glamour, and absolutely no pay. But things seem to be turning around a little as more and more men find themselves taking over the responsibilities of the home. I've recently found myself among their number. When my wife returned to work, I abandoned my construction business to tackle a one-year-old, a shopping list, a dirty toilet, and the laundry piling up. I'm not going to bore you with another cute "Mr. Mom" story full of observations that women have been making for thousands of years — namely that raising small children is a complex and moving experience, housework is demanding and endless, and presoaking problem stains really does make the whites whiter and the colors brighter. I'd like to avoid the obvious and talk instead about how I've applied some of my housebuilding experience to homemaking, and how homemaking might benefit my construction career should I ever return to it.

Since I brought up the subject of laundry, let's take a look at a new approach to that nagging nemesis of housewives everywhere: static cling. It's only recently that I've begun to appreciate what a pain in the pants this really is. Socks are welded to sweaters, and nylon turtlenecks spring into little balls as soon as you spread them out on the table to fold. I realize this problem can be neatly skirted with those little blue perfumed foam rubber things you throw in the drier, but that's too easy. My male training and blue-collar experience won't allow me to use those in good conscience.

Instead I've chosen to apply the little bit I've learned about the dynamics of electricity while in the trades. Now, static electricity isn't exactly house current. You can't just unplug it, you have to ground it out. Anyone who's ever touched a water faucet on a dry winter day will understand what I'm talking about. So I thought this grounding principle could be applied to the problem of static cling. I tied one end of a copper ground wire to a rivet on a pair of 501s and the other end to the drier's metal spinner. I started 'er up and in less than a minute found the clothes wound up with that wire tighter than a hay bale. So I tried another method. I removed the wad of supercharged clothing from the drier, put my arms around it, and headed on out to the living room. I shuffled my feet up and down the carpet until I figured the laundry and I had become one unified charge, then I went and touched the door knob. It made a loud snap and stung like crazy, but did absolutely nothing for the laundry. Obviously this couldn't work, and you'd be stupid to try it, but there are other innovative methods I've applied to my housework that do make things easier.

We all know how much time homemakers waste trying to clean house and keep young children out of harm's way at the same time. They rush around from one poison cleaning product to the next, making sure not to leave one out where the kid can get at it. They must use the bowl cleaner, put it away, grab the cleanser, put it away, and on and on until a twenty-minute job takes up to two hours or more. Well, I've found a way around all of this.

I dug out my old tool belt with the leather multi-pouches, hammer loops, and shoulder harness. On my right I have the Comet in one pouch alongside the Drāno, with a scratch pad and a dust cloth where the tape rule used to go. On the other side is the Windex and furniture polish with a squeegie stuck in the hammer loop. That leaves one whole pocket and a few small nail pouches for Baby's favorite toys, a change of diapers, some salve, cookies, and a spare bib or two. Now I can clean the whole house, serve my child's every need, and get dinner started without retracing a step. I've already read the paper and clipped half my sale ads before my wife walks through the door. Professional efficiency. That's the way to go.

Then there's one thing I learned around the house that I wish I'd known about out in the field. In construction a guy finds himself coming home with some toxic substance or another spread from his fingertips to his elbows, and nothing short of gasoline will usually take care of it. Now I've found a better way.

I cleaned out the wood stove one day and ended up with hands blacker than Dad's fried eggs. I scrubbed and scraped with every poison I could find, but nothing seemed to cut it. So I went ahead and made dinner anyway. That's how I stumbled onto my discovery. I found that no matter how dirty the hands or how persistent the dirt, making a meat loaf will clean you up slicker than a wet kid. Working the raw meat and soda crackers between the fingers for a couple minutes will erase anything from chimney soot to furniture oil. I tell you, it saved my day, and if you'd ever tasted my meat loaf, you'd admit the added seasoning couldn't hurt anything.

You can see that my transition from housebuilder to homemaker has been fairly painless. I'm the laundry-doin'est, counter-wipin'est, baby-boucin'est little dad you ever laid eyes on. Sure, it's hard work, but it's the challenge I like. Innovation, experimentation, that's the stuff of professionalism, and I have every intention of being the best in my chosen trade.

Now, if I could figure out how a guy can get paid for doing this . . .

Dish
Demeanor

Household controversies range from church of choice to the color of the new family car. But nothing on the long list of excuses for domestic disturbance can produce so much fuss as the proper way to wash a dish. Dish-washing techniques are as many and varied as the floral designs on Melmac plates and are surpassed only by bathroom habits in their inflexibility. You can tell a person by his dish-washing style, but as I say, you can't tell him very much.

Dish washers can be broken into two basic categories. There are *Wash-and-Driers,* who methodically wash a few, dry a few, wash a few, dry a few, put some away, start over, and when they're done, they're done. All the rest are *Wash-and-Drippers*. They wash the whole pile, then stack the dishes precariously in a rubber drainer until the next morning. Wash-and-Driers show a basic insecurity in not being able to leave things go. They're the same folks who can spot a dustball under the sofa from across the room and won't relax until it's swept up. Wash-and-Driers normally work in teams, which can promote marital harmony, but which can also lead to whole new points of contention by allowing two solid opinions near the same small sink. Whereas one partner might want to do the silverware first to get it out of the way, the other will surely prefer to let it soak to make the job a little easier. There is a point of agreement, however, among all dish washers, and it's that everyone hates to do silverware.

Wash-and-Drippers are the free spirits of the kitchen, and can be divided into two subgroups: *right-brained stackers* and *left-brained stackers*. Right-brained stackers will randomly clean cup, plate, or serving spoon without regard to shape or size and creatively teeter them on one another until a dish-sculpture rivaling anything in the modern arts takes form at sinkside. This is all well and good, but it requires a municipal bomb squad to dismantle the stack without breaking anything or waking up the baby. Right-brained stackers of the Wash-and-Dripper persuasion reveal a basic love of expression and are the poets and painters of the twin sink. Picasso was a notorious dish stacker, and his *Crystal Goblet on Salad Tongs in Blue Bowl* stands to this day as the quintessential right-brained dish stack.

Left-brained Wash-and-Drippers would build a good bridge or a level house if given the opportunity. They choose their next dirty dish with care, basing their selections on size, weight, and shape with no regard to order of appearance. Lefties wash cast-iron skillets and large ceramic bowls well ahead of the bone china, so as the stack grows the weight bears on the hardier pieces. No left-brained stacker would ever hang a bowl on a wineglass stem or leave the blades of sharp knives pointing up. They might, however, in their zeal for orderliness, stack dishes so close together that even a day later wet plates can be found tightly layered at the bottom of the drainer. This drives right-brained stackers absolutely bonkers, because being dedicated Wash-and-Drippers, they wouldn't put a towel to a dish at gunpoint.

If an argument isn't had over *how* the dishes are to be washed, one will surely come over *when*. Many married and most all single dish owners are famous procrastinators when it comes to this chore, and some have been known to put it off until there is not an adequate cup or plate left in the house. Once the last empty peanut-butter jar has been drunk from, one of two things takes place. The first is to set aside a rainy weekend to scrape, sort, sanitize, and stack the mountain of tableware. The second and more common practice is to sublet or sell the house.

On the flip side of these casual washers are the folks who virtually clean as they go. We've all been witness to the host who rinses out your coffee cup between servings and has it washed, dried, and hung on a hook before the last swallow reaches your belly. These people, when left to their own devices, would choose to eat their meals over the garbage disposal rather than soil a plate or stain a fork. They scour their sinks with neurotic regularity, and finding a noodle dangling from the bottom of a drain-stopper is likely to send them into convulsions. Invariably alone at the end, most *Clean-as-They-Goers* marry but lose their spouses, sometimes to mental institutions, but mostly to well-adjusted slobs.

I believe my wife was quite fortunate in finding herself a well-adjusted slob the first time around. As we are both of the Wash-and-Dripper right-brained stacker persuasion, we have very few cleanup confrontations. In fact, what we have is a healthy competition. We take turns marveling at the sinkside sculptures each devises with his or her stacking skill. We're a pretty even match on this point, and had assumed this playful rivalry would go on forever. Unfortunately we've run into a problem.

Feeling exceptionally inspired one recent evening, I took it upon myself to use our wedding glasses as the foundation for a dish stack of unprecedented ambition. We had several guests for dinner and managed to use every piece of decent tableware in the house, so I was able to arrange them one on top of the other with a ten-pound iron soup kettle at the summit. It's a marvel of balance and fragility with a certain air of grace juxtaposed by the presence of the soup pot.

Picasso himself might have awarded me a spirited slap in the pants with a damp dish rag at the sight of it. The problem is that we're afraid to touch the thing. Those wineglasses, the very symbol of our unity, are holding up every dish in the kitchen. Neither one of us is willing to risk their demise by dismantling my creation. It's going on a week now, and might go on forever. Who knows how long it'll stay standing, but in the meantime, it gives us something to talk about while we scrape the paper plates.

PART
·2·

SMALL
COMFORTS

❖

Small
Comfort

L ast year my life found me on some pretty long walks in
some pretty big cities, and on most of them I came
across street people. I don't mean people who love the
street. I mean people who live in the street. Homeless indigents, bums, winos, derelicts. Whatever you want to call
them, there they are, crouched in doorways, sprawled on
bus benches, and peering from alleyways. I don't get to big
cities often, so I don't come across them as much as some
do.

Those who meet up with them all the time are better
at walking around them than I am. They can pass them up
without an ear or eye open. If they feel anything like com-
passion, they can veil it just enough to appear honestly in-
different. I found that hard to do, but getting caught up in
the big-city way of things, I kept practicing. I quit looking
over at them and stopped straining to hear their pleas for
money above the traffic noise. I quit trying to peer into
their beggar cans to see if anybody else had put coins in

them. I quit reading their signs asking for jobs, money, food, and help. I started to get pretty good at it.

After a day or two on the streets of Washington, D.C., I could walk dead through DuPont Circle and not trip over my heartstrings if an old man called out for change. I could wave off the aggressive vagrants with one quick backhand motion. I'd look past these people for some far-off sign or building to focus my direction on. By golly, I was getting cosmopolitan and enjoying it. I'd mastered the subway. I'd learned to time my street crossings so as not to appear flustered or hurried. And now I'd gotten rid of any guilt or intimidation I'd ever felt at being a well-dressed white boy in the presence of poverty. What a thrill to stand defiantly on the street surveying my options, just as cool, calm, and numb as a post.

I carried on this way for a while, but then something broke me.

It was getting way past lunch on a free day. My stomach was rumbling, and I was out in search of an interesting place to grab a knockwurst and a beer. I turned a corner and there in a doorway crouched an old man with a block-lettered sign on his chest. It said simply, I'M HUNGRY. I'd seen signs like this before, but this guy *looked* hungry, really hungry, and tired to the bone. With my stomach as empty as his tin can, that simple statement, "I'm hungry," took on new worth.

It struck me as if hearing my little son cry like the weight of all the world was crushing down on his tiny shoulders. I'd drag myself across hot coals to comfort him, and I couldn't pass by this old soul. Two doors down was an Arthur Treacher's Fish and Chips restaurant. "Don't give him money," I thought. "It could get stole from him, or he might just drink it away. Go buy the guy a bag of fish and a cup of coffee. What'll it cost, three bucks?"

I started in the door just as five young businesspeople came out, and I had to stand aside for a moment. That killed it. The self-satisfied expressions on those successful young faces snapped whatever I had going with that old man. As I watched them file past him, preoccupied with their own conversation, I felt the old indifference coming back. I suddenly felt more of their fold than the beggar's, and I moved away from the door.

"Nobody feeds street people," I thought. "What are you doing? Who are you trying to impress?"

As I looked back at the old man, he happened to turn his head and look at me. I was found out. He realized what I was up to. He knew I was wavering and held my gaze. I'd only seen that look in eyes once before. That was in the eyes of a deer I'd dropped but not quite killed while hunting in Southeast Alaska. As I walked up to the dying animal to finish it, there was that same pitiful look of appeal. Every cell in that deer's body hoped beyond hope that I'd change my mind and walk away.

I didn't walk away then, but I did that day in Washington. Walked away clean. I strolled down the street defiant and numb as a post. The only indication of a crack in my composure was the blood in my cheeks and my hands dug deep in my pockets like I'd never pull them out. I could feel that old man's stare burning at the base of my neck, but I wouldn't turn around.

I came back home to Alaska shortly after that day, and I don't see street people anymore. I eat well, all my friends eat well, and I forget about that old guy a lot. Sometimes at night, though, my little son wakes me with cries like the weight of all the world is crushing down on his tiny shoulders. I hold him tight, rock him, and think how I'll never be able to look that old man in the eye again. Not even in my sleep.

Realizing this is no great comfort to anyone.

Gross
Estimates

Americans have got to be the most anticipated people on earth. Everyplace we look there's the results of this poll or that survey. It's estimated this, predicted that, or early indications of the other thing. It's like having some guy come to dinner and keep telling you, "Now wait, I know what you're going to say," before you open your mouth, or, "I knew you were going to feel that way about it," after you do. And the worst of all is the "See how you are?" when you do something you've always done and he thinks he's clever because he notices it. Nobody can stand these kinds of people in their private lives, and I don't know why we put up with it in public.

Of course, all these polls and surveys are designed to find out which way we're heading so they can ambush us with stupid products we don't need, television minidramas we can't follow, and made-to-order politicians. They start those opinion polls about a year before an election. They ask what qualities you look for in a leader, what issues you would like to see addressed, and how you think the leader should address the issues you would like to see addressed. Come time for the primaries — *whammo!* — there he is, Mr. Right. All bought and paid for.

I suppose there is an estimate somewhere on how many people spend their time estimating people, and my estimate is that we can stand every one of them right on their ear.

The next time a polltaker calls your house, give him the wrong answers. If you want to say Democrat, say Republican. If you mean yes, say no. Don't do this on every single question or we'll get caught up in another prediction. Estimates will show that Americans are becoming wiseguys. Be subtle and we can ring bells in every capital and industry.

When you're at the store, don't pick up the roll of paper towels they tell us has the biggest bounce. None of them bounce. Grab the cheapest roll and go. You're just going to wipe up a mess with it and throw it away, so who cares? And some of these books. You know the ones. They come off the presses with "Number One Best Seller" already stamped on the cover because the publishers are that sure we'll buy them. Let's don't. Who really needs to burn through another international thriller? Innocent man or woman is caught up in something bigger than his or her self. It's up to our hero to (A) win the war, (B) preserve democracy, (C) save the world, or (D) provide titillating sexual fantasy to the masses. Flash scene of Berlin Wall, trench coat, romantic encounter on Lake Geneva, then on to startling conclusion where neo-Nazi conspiracy is exposed through employment of sheer wits, high morals, and the stiletto depicted on the cover dripping blood all over a swastika and a lace brassiere. See, you've heard the story, so skip it next time and buy a psychology textbook or a *House-plants Illustrated* instead. Market analyzers will go nuts trying to figure it out.

You people with the Nielsen rating machines on your televisions should turn them to the public station and leave them there. Watch "Dynasty" and *Blue Thunder* out in the garage on the portable if you have to. It'll only be for a while. It shouldn't take very long. We'll have them pounding their heads on their computer monitors before you can say "trend report."

Just imagine the hundreds of high-level emergency board meetings that will be called to order across the nation. Power brokers, king makers, empire builders, and soda-pop tycoons, every one of them poking at a tender ulcer and asking, "What in the heck are they up to out there?"

We'll never tell. Not until it's over. I want to see Tom Brokaw's face on the evening news as he announces that "The American public is showing a tendency to have no tendencies. Conjecture at eleven."

Once the opinion pollsters and market surveyors have lost their jobs and found honest work counting spawned-out salmon in the Yukon River, we can relax and go back to normal, our point well made.

We'll talk to them in language they understand. Any good businessman will tell you that the advantage lies in being unpredictable. I want those people to look out their upper-story boardroom windows at the milling crowds below, and admit, "Ladies and gentlemen, we have to watch these folks. They're pretty tricky."

Senior Boom

We Baby Boomers were officially spawned during the years 1946 to 1964, and have become, without a doubt, one of the most influential bits of humanity to hit the streets since the Mongol horde swept across Asia. Leaving hula hoops, the Monkees, miniskirts, and underenrolled universities in our wake, we've now progressed to BABY ON BOARD stickers and well-tended stock portfolios. Due to sheer weight of numbers, we get almost everything we want. If we're not sure what we want, there is always some demographic genius out there to show us something we never thought of. If you can figure out a product that the Baby Boomers will buy, you can look forward to early retirement. And that's exactly what the merchants and producers are thinking about, retirement. Our retirement.

You see, it finally dawned on somebody that the boomers ain't babies no more, and are getting less like them every day. Some of us are already in the throes of middle age and nearing the halfway point in our working careers. As we speak, manufacturers of products for the elderly are gearing up for our expected demands when we all decide we're old. Their plans aren't exactly in the public domain yet, but I've managed to find out a few of the things they have in store for us.

I hear that one orthopedic shoe company is planning expansive additions to their facilities, including ten acres of new corrective-sole storage. Some thirty new assembly lines will soon start punching out plain black creepers, and one of the cane conglomerates is stockpiling bamboo walking sticks with little rubber tips. Geritol will soon upgrade its packaging to add a little pizzazz to the experience of being old and worn out. The denture industry is fairly drooling at the prospects of the early twenty-first century. I'd like to suggest they all settle down and think things through for a minute.

The odds of us growing into ordinary old folks are about the same as Jane Fonda running on the Republican ticket with George Bush. I have a feeling we will have about as much use for orthopedic shoes as we did for Lawrence Welk. Baby Boomers as a group have singled themselves out as one of the most self-indulgent generations in history. No new generation likes to do things the way their parents did, but because there are so many of us, we don't do things the way our parents did in the biggest way. Granted there is nothing we can do about getting old, but I have every confidence we are going to do it with our typical flare for contrariness.

For one thing, the health and fitness craze might well assure many of us very long and productive old ages (unless, as I suspect, we find that running aimlessly around in parks during our prime did little but use us up early). We'll see about that, but we're bound to live longer than earlier generations anyway because that's the trend and the medicine men get smarter every day. For this reason there is going to be a whole lot of old boomers around for a long long time. We're going to make an institution out of being over the hill. In just a couple of decades, it's going to be so popular to be an old fart that everybody's going to wanna be one. All I can say is, the marketplace better get ready for us.

Adidas and Reebok better get their heads together on an ankle-support running shoe. Levi's should be planning their shrink-to-fits to shrink a little less as we all fill out. Unpopular sizes like, say, a 42 waist and 28 inseam are going to be pretty hot items before Calvin Klein knows what hit him.

If you own shares in Ex-Lax, you'd be well advised to hang on to them, but only if they do something about the flavors. Something in an Almond Mocha or Swiss Cream would seem appropriate. Same goes for the smell of Vicks, and while we're on the subject, if the medicos don't come up with a cure for rheumatism pretty quick, they're going to have a riot on their hands.

Fashion and entertainment best get ready for a plunge into the past. It's been observed that old people tend toward the styles and sounds of their misspent youth. Grandma loves those old seventy-eights and her print cotton nightgown circa 1910. Muzak had better get those 1,000 Strings renditions of Barry Manilow tunes out of the nursing homes, put some Creedence Clearwater in there, and turn it up. Big-screen TVs around the mineral baths will be seeing a lot of the old Woodstock footage, and *The Big Chill* is destined to replace *Gone With the Wind* as the classic film of choice.

I don't know if getting old necessarily means we'll all turn ornery, but I plan to. I look forward to dusting off some old radical politics and letting my white hair grow over my shoulders just to irritate neo-neo-conservative children who I know won't come to visit. I want to drive too slow in a '68 VW with a rainbow sticker in the window and speakers in the back. I'll wait too long at stoplights and flash menacing gestures at hyperactive upstarts behind me who don't like it. This is going to be great.

Of course I could be wrong about all of this. We may end up just getting old and quiet. We might decide that gin rummy, shuffleboard, and some light gardening are just the thing to fill the golden years with. We could come to think that red jogging shoes look ridiculous on the ends of shaky legs and big, dumb black ones are just the ticket. If we have any hearing left, we might choose not to further threaten it with more loud music. A few thousand strings doink-doinking out a favorite old melody in the background may do just as well. In short, we may all find out by the time we're eighty-five that being sensible is the better way to go. Is that possible? I'm not sure, kids, but I have great faith in us, and I just don't think so.

Mental Safety

Consumer advocates have for years been trying to protect us from ourselves. They've succeeded in saving us from a myriad of hazardous products from the Pinto to pajamas that burst into flames on contact with a warm thought. It seems that making anything small enough to pass between a baby's lips is now against the law, and everything we buy to eat short of tap water has to be hermetically sealed. My stepladder is burdened with so many instructions and warning labels that I can hardly pack it up the stairs (stairs which must be outfitted with an approved handrail as required by state law).

I'm not complaining about this. Even though a few new rules stretch the limits of reason, I have to admit this is a somewhat safer world than the one I grew up in. We're all going to live longer, and we owe a lot of that to the consumer advocates. If I have a problem with their work, it's that they are not addressing all there is at fault with manufactured products. Safety is a biggie, for sure — nobody wants to spend his hard-earned dollars on a death wish. Value is also a grand consideration — it's getting harder and harder to spot a rip-off in an economy that can't even decide what a dollar's worth. But there's a whole lot more to a good buy than a safe product for a fair price. There is a mental health quotient also at stake here.

Psychiatrists have recently coined a new term, *Agent Blue*. It refers to whatever it is behind the drastic increase in depression, violence, and suicide in our society. Now, I'm not at all sure, but I think I have an idea of what a great big part of this Agent Blue is, and it's something our consumer raiders should investigate. I'm talking about bad ideas embedded in good products. There's a lot of stuff in this world that we all long for, require, and use that has a certain amount of misery built into it.

Take, for example, the tags in some clothing. I have a pair of long johns I paid close to twenty bucks for. They are of some state-of-the-art fabric that is warm, durable, and so comfortable I feel like I'm climbing into bed every time I put them on. But there was this tag in the back. It was made out of something just short of stainless steel and gave me the sensation of having a piece of shattered flowerpot down my britches. I tore it out after the first wear.

That opened up a whole new bag of worms. The tag had been sewn on with about two thousand stitches per inch, and although the tag was gone, the stitching remained. It provided all the comfort of a serrated knife sawing away at my fourth lumbar. No amount of chewing and slashing would get rid of the stuff. So I have to wear my new long johns inside out.

Now why would a company produce a garment of such obvious merit, then booby-trap it with a thing like that? It's either a KGB conspiracy or there's a very bitter person at the helm of some sewing machine. Whichever it is, it's irritating, and should be looked into.

While on the subject of garments, there's another little mystery that for years has contributed nothing to my peace of mind, namely the tendency of the pant legs on Levi's to migrate. After several washings, the side seams are screwed around so far it looks like your legs are welded on crooked. If you haven't noticed, they're not giving Levi's away these days, and we're paying substantial amounts of dough to look like genetic misfits. It's a little thing to be sure, but it might be just these little things behind our deteriorating mental condition.

Luckily we live in a potentially just world, and there are compromises to be made that could relieve some of the tension.

For years I've been looking for a glue that might actually work. We've had super glues, crazy glues, wonder glues, mighty glues, and easy glues, but precious few glues that stick. I recently bought a new soup pot, and it came, of course, with a label stuck to it. This label refuses to go away. I've scrubbed it, boiled it, scraped it, applied every toxic chemical known to a kitchen to it, and it endures. More than a few times over the last two weeks I've wiped my brow and exclaimed, "What kind of glue did they use on this thing?"

Now, here's my compromise. If the gluemakers would sell us whatever it is keeping that label on my soup pot, and if the pot manufacturer would in turn use any other trade glue on its labels, we would live in a near-perfect world. The things I glued together would stay stuck, and the labels on cookware would gracefully fall off before I got them home from the store.

What's *your* gripe? Potato-chip bags that blow out at the bottom while you're trying to open the top? Impenetrable peanut packages on airlines? Could we cut down on airborne violence if we didn't have to carry knives to get at the snack? Why do you have to pull the engine of some Italian cars to change their spark plugs? For that matter, why are Fiats listed on the Foreign Trade Exchange under "Durable Goods"? These questions need to be answered.

Write your congressman. Call Nader. Boycott. Do whatever it takes. Just don't sit around thinking because a baby can't choke on it, or you can't fall off of it, that it's okay. A baby couldn't choke on an Edsel, and you couldn't fall off a pair of 501s and get hurt very bad. But I hope you see the hidden danger here.

Look every potential purchase over carefully. Read the side of the box. If it appears to contain even a little Agent Blue, remember: it's a bargain at no price, and unsafe at any speed.

I Aim
to Please

It's pretty obvious that Americans can't find enough things to spend their money on. Pet rocks, fifty-dollar rag dolls, Dodge trucks — the list goes on and on. People will pay for darn near anything if it's sold properly. The problem is just thinking up stuff to sell. Every time I hear of some brilliant new con, I kick myself for not thinking of it first. I've always fancied myself a bit of a businessman, and it irks me to see somebody else beat me to the punch.

When I was out East, someone showed me a tin can which the label claimed was full of "Fresh Maine Air." What a great scam. I've seen the cans of what they try to sell to tourists around here as "Gold Pan Material" — it's actually dirt and gravel, but it is canned *something*. In Maine some freethinking entrepreneur has found a way to sell *empty* cans to people. Why didn't I think of that?

We've got pretty nice air around here too, and canning lines that sit idle most of the year. "Fresh Alaska Air" would drive Maine air right off the market. I'd go through with it, but I hate to steal ideas, and the high overhead of Alaska canning operations would make it cost-prohibitive. I thought about having the cans made in Thailand at lower prices, but feared the class action suit that would surely come if someone were to discover that what was billed as a whiff of pure arctic air turned out to be a snootfull of downtown Bangkok. I put the whole business aside and was scheming some more when I heard someone had aced me again.

"Adopt-a-Ghost" it's called. Kind of a cross between a Cabbage Patch Doll and absolutely nothing. Your ghost comes with a name and brief character description so you know how to act around it. I don't know if it comes in a can too, but that seems like a pretty handy way to package a spook. Casper in a can. Americans *love* things in cans. They might offer three convenient sizes, one to suit every household's ectoplasmic needs. It's a tremendous idea that's humbling by its sheer genius.

I was desperate to get with the program and think up something to sell America when it came to me in the middle of a beer commercial: we love to be flattered. That's how they sell us all that junk — they make us feel good about ourselves for buying it.

So what I've decided to do is bypass the products altogether and sell pure sweet flattery. Everybody wants some recognition. You too, right?

How about for twenty bucks I name my dog after you for a day? Wouldn't it be swell to know I'd spend a whole day calling for Chuck, Kirby, or Bob? Bend down to scratch his ears and say, "Good dog, Bill." Put out the food bowl with a "Here ya go, Stephanie." (Women's names are okay because he's been neutered and doesn't care about that too much.) You'll also receive a Polaroid snapshot of me and the dog with your name written on it someplace, and the satisfaction of knowing that for a full twenty-four hours you've had a namesake.

There's no end to this business. Send me ten dollars and I'll start nice rumors about you. For five bucks I'll ask you where you bought your hat, or who cuts your hair. And for a dollar — that's right, one dollar — I'll put your name on my "Good Guys" list and leave it on the coffee table to browse through at my leisure.

So get on the stick and buy yourself some strokes. I think you folks are the cat's meow. (That one was on the house.)

Miss America

I watched the Miss America contest this year. I don't remember when I last saw one, but nothing much has changed. There was the same middle-aged emcee doting on the hopefuls, the current Miss America bubbling over last year's magic moment, and of course the final ten contestants in attack formation smiling their best Ultra-Brite smiles. I read somewhere that they put Vaseline on their teeth so they don't dry out and get their lips stuck to them. Good idea. It wouldn't look good to give a teary-eyed promise to spend the rest of your life benefiting needy families in Appalachia by singing operettas in a bathing suit if your lips were stuck in some idiotic grin. They've thought of everything.

It appeared as though they'd all had their vertebrae surgically fused so that the only moving parts were legs that propelled them along at an ideal linear speed, like a fleet of golf carts. Their heads turned smartly from side to side, and their hands rose up to wave in that mechanical back-and-forth motion as if working some huge control knob. In a sense, I guess, that's what they were doing.

Young women all over the country were looking up to this group for inspiration. Out of these ten would come one Miss America, the quintessential young single American female. College-educated, career-oriented, fashion-conscious, and built like a five-hundred-dollar privy.

Each gave us her little biography and ambitions. "I'm a senior at Backwater U. majoring in Communication. I hope one day to head up public relations for large charity organizations that help *all* the people of the world. Until then, please take note of my lovely breasts and mole-free shoulder blades. Thank you."

As the house applause faded to a styling mousse commercial, I couldn't help but wonder if anybody was buying all this. I pictured an Adrienne in Des Moines. She's not painting her nails, she's biting them wondering if she's going to make the rent this month. She works part time at the phone company and takes night classes in computer science. Someday she's going to make enough money to get out of this town and take a job on the West Coast. Get away from all her bozo boyfriends and get a new car. Then she might do something different with her hair and look into world hunger. For now, she can't afford to do either. In fact, she couldn't afford to do much of anything this Saturday night but watch this stupid pageant on TV and chain-smoke cigarettes to stay on her diet.

And there were our ten beauties lined up and waiting for the judges' decision. Hundred-dollar hairdos enshrined in lacquer. Makeup from petroleum by-products to take the edge off the bright stage lights. Skillfully applied lip gloss outlining skillfully applied smiles. There were enough complex carbon molecules wafting off the group that Adrienne couldn't safely light a cigarette within a hundred yards of there.

All these thoughts entered my mind as I waited for the grand finale, that moment when Adrienne and I and the rest of the country would be given our next Miss America. The artificial smiles would give way to the weeping passion of victory or the scowl of defeat.

Then the most amazing thing happened, or failed to happen, I should say. It made me wonder what I've missed since I saw my last beauty contest. Miss America didn't cry. She accepted her crown and marched down the runway dry-eyed and confident. None of the cute pouts I've come to expect. No trembling lips choking back tears of amazement at becoming everything she'd ever wanted to be. I felt cheated of the pleasure of seeing that overwhelming flush people get when they've won true fame and fortune. It wasn't "Little ol' me?"; it was "You bet it's me." A true child of the eighties firmly grabbing another rung on a well-designed career ladder.

Watching her make her way down the runway held all the emotional appeal of seeing a new car roll off the assembly line. Adrienne walks around it, looking it over. She opens the glove box and looks at the manufacturer's sticker. MADE IN AMERICA. Ain't she a beauty?

Lost Mail

Acts of God occur everywhere, but nowhere with as much frequency as on the high seas. One of His more recent performances was to bounce around a container barge on thirty-foot seas in the Gulf of Alaska. That made for a lot of water in all the wrong places, and, sure enough, some cargo got lost in it.

No big deal, really; it happens all the time. But there was something about this cargo that caught my interest. It seems that a whole container of U.S. mail went overboard and, presumably, sank. That hardly sounds earth-shaking either, but what got me going was the Postal Service announcement acknowledging that 20,680 pounds of mail was lost. It seemed like such a strange way to put it. Before then, I'd never really thought of mail by the pound. I'd get a little mail, or a lot of mail. Sometimes I'd get a stack of it, or, after returning from a long trip, a pile would be waiting for me. But I've yet to ask my wife if we got any mail and hear her say, "Oh, only about eight ounces." Of course that's all changed now.

Since this came up I've been guessing the weight of my mail. You'd be surprised how light it is. Even counting magazines and free samples, I figure I average about four pounds a week. That's when it hit me what a catastrophe losing this container of mail really was. Twenty thousand, six hundred and eighty pounds of mail is a lot of mail. Based on four pounds a week, that's ninety-nine years' worth. How'd you like not to get your mail for a whole century? Another way of looking at it would be to assume we each get about four pounds a week. That container represented a week of mail to over five thousand people. Now, that's a tragedy.

Just think of it. All those little "I love you, Grandma" refrigerator drawings lost to the briny deep. Picture a "Dear Oliver, if you don't answer me this time I'll know we're finally through" returning to pulp on the ocean floor. Imagine "I know it's stupid to send cash, Phil, but I didn't have time to get a money order" being sucked in and spit out by an irritated halibut. Sentiments lost, relationships ruined, and friendships strained. And that's not even counting the merchandise.

Alaskans live by mail-order catalogues. Somewhere in the Japanese Current we now have little schools of L. L. Bean sweaters, Sears bed linen, Eddie Bauer boot liners, and personalized note pads by Spencer Gifts all headed with the salmon fry for the high seas. What's the Soviet trawler captain going to think when his crew shows him the "Rambo Commie Basher" doll they dredged up that morning? It could touch off a serious international incident.

Just as I was really starting to slip into a dither over this whole mess, I took another long, hard look at my last four pounds of mail. It consisted of a women's underwear catalogue, a catalogue of gifts for gifted children, three magazine renewal notices, a sweepstakes, two political action committee newsletters (one left, one right), and a life insurance offer from J. C. Penney.

There was nothing there. Except for the underwear catalogue, there wasn't a keeper in the bunch, and the only reason any of it made it to my desk was so I could figure out how much it weighed. Judging from the amount of real mail I get as opposed to the other kind, I figure I get about a pound of the good stuff for every ton of the other kind. Using this formula, there were probably only ten or eleven letters on that barge. That really helped me to put this thing in perspective and cope with this tragedy on the high seas.

Twenty thousand, six hundred and eighty pounds of U.S. mail lost forever. Big deal.

Chain
Reactions

I got a strange letter in the mail today. It's one of those Xeroxed chain letters, and I have no idea who sent it to me. The purpose of this letter is not to make money or collect recipes; it's to spread good luck. I'm supposed to make twenty copies of the thing and send them out within four days. It says to send them to friends and associates I think might need good luck. Like I don't think everybody could use a little.

The letter starts out: "Kiss someone you love and make magic" — as opposed to kissing someone else and making time, I guess. It goes on to detail the success stories of a few of its previous recipients. A guy in the air force received seventy grand for cooperating, and another guy named Joe got forty grand but lost it when he broke the chain. Gene Welch lost his dog, tragically, after receiving the letter and failing to pass it on, but here's the good news, he got seven thousand some-odd dollars before its death. Good for you, Gene.

It tells about a guy who received the letter in 1953 and won a two-million-dollar lottery. Another guy got the letter but mislaid it. He lost his job, then found the letter, mailed his twenty copies, and was given a better job. Right, we get the picture.

The whole thing seemed pretty harmless and just a little silly until I got to the last line: "Dalan Fairchild received the letter and, not believing, threw it away. Nine days later he died."

Oh, now, this is just great. A letter that started out inviting me to kiss someone and make magic is now threatening to kill me if I don't play along. To get rid of this curse, I gotta go pay twenty cents a copy at a Xerox machine, buy four and a half bucks' worth of stamps, and pass the curse on to twenty of my friends. I don't know who sent this letter to me, but I think a little more of my friends than to lay a deal like this on them, even if I am superstitious. It seems like they get enough guilt, fear, and anxiety from their regular suppliers without me sending along unsolicited free samples.

I picture some poor twisted soul sweating in a walk-up apartment in L.A. He's close to tears and has just about had it with everything and everybody. As he polishes his rifle and contemplates the unspeakable, the postman pushes an envelope through the slot in his door. "Kiss somebody and make magic. . . ." By the time he gets to the end of the letter all remaining strands of sanity are severed and we get a big headline in the morning paper. Like I say, people don't need this kind of anxiety floating around loose.

Besides, this whole thing doesn't make mathematical sense. If somebody did get this letter in 1953 like they say, then it's been around for a while. Assume for a minute that everyone in the pyramid did what they were supposed to and sent along twenty copies within four days. It would take only a little over a month before the number of letters in circulation exceeded the number of people that exist by some five times over.

So who gets all the leftover good luck? Could this be a scam after all? Maybe it's some international conspiracy of casino owners trying to water down all the good luck in the world until none of us has any worth mentioning.

The letter tells us that some missionary in South America named Saul Anthony DeCroff originated this scheme. He may have worked out the math on this thing too. You can bet that with twenty-five billion letters in circulation, sooner or later somebody's bound to either win a car or drop dead within four days of getting one. That makes good ol' Saul DeCroff look pretty clever. But to what end? I don't know what church he's working for down there, but they better call him back to headquarters. The good reverend's been in the jungle too long.

I'm assuming that you've received this letter too. If I got one, then everybody did. If that's so, then listen up here. Don't rush off to Kopy Kwik. Don't give in to fear. I have a better idea.

Instead of spending what would amount to around eight bucks on Xerox machines and postage to perpetuate this hogwash, keep four bucks for yourself, buy something for your sweetheart, and send the other four bucks to me. If there's as many of you out there as I think there are, we will become one of the largest financial concerns in the world overnight. Trust me, I worked it out on my calculator.

Since I do have a calculator, I'm probably the best one

to manage our corporate holdings. I'll only withdraw enough to cover my basic administrative costs and what I'll need to keep up the limos and Lear jets. You'll get a nice letter every quarter, or as soon as I get to it, letting you know how things are going and asking if there's anything in particular you'd like me to buy, like Yellowstone Park, or Vermont. As a stockholder, you'll get into these places free of charge.

Your dedicated chief executive will keep it a personal organization. I'll send you pictures of my kid as he grows up and maybe a nice card around the holidays.

This sounds like just another scheme, I know, but I'll bet you twenty postage stamps it's more than you're going to get out of that chain letter.

Burger
Blues

This is an embarrassing thing to admit, but the first place I ever ate at in Alaska was a McDonald's restaurant. That was in Fairbanks eleven years ago. I found it hysterical that I could get to faraway Fairbanks and find a Big Mac dispensary at my service. I ate there just to say I did and took note of the sign on the door claiming it was only the second McDonald's in the whole state.

I'm reminded of this lately by the construction of our very own McBurger stand right here at the end of the road. Whatever I found so amusing about that second-only Alaska McDonald's escapes me now. People here take the appearance of this and other fast-food joints very personally. An invasion of their privacy.

McDonald's has come to represent everything bad that is happening to Alaska. It's all blamed on the newcomers from everyplace else. The golden arches are an easy symbol for "Everyplace Else." That's where all the surly cowboys with crude oil under their fingernails come from. That's where carpetbagger developers come from. For God's sake, that's where *tourists* come from.

It's also the place where I and a whole scad of other born-again Alaskans come from. "Outside," we call it, and there's hardly one of us didn't try to pull the door shut behind him on the way in. It's pretty typical, really. For being the most adaptable critters in all God's creation, we sure do kick and scream when somebody tries to change things.

We've all got our little ideas about what Alaska is and should be, and we want it kept just that way. I had an old-timer tell me once that Alaska is being able to piss off your own front porch, and if it ever got to the point where, by God, he couldn't, then he would pack it in. I suppose he's still around. You can still pee off your front porch here if you're so inclined and your house points the right way. But there are other things not so easy anymore. Longevity bonuses and local hire laws are going the way of home marijuana crops. Alaskans are having a heck of a time accepting that the U.S. Constitution applies to them too.

Anchorage has some of the worst air pollution in the nation and cradles our very own TV preachers and homeless indigents. Rising high above it all are the golden arches, twin monuments to banality. "Over Fifty Billion Served," it says. My God, that's more than the pipeline serves and it's all in burgers.

It seemed like such an impossible number that I had to figure out how big it really was. I did some arithmetic, counted up all the zeros, and found that fifty billion hamburgers would cover one square mile twenty-three feet deep. That's not taking into account the ones on the bottom being all squashed together. The thought of it disgusted me.

I looked over our beautiful Kachemak Bay landscape and imagined this blight of ground meat and food additives sitting on it. Then it struck me. You wouldn't even have to see it. There's about forty crevasses I can count from here that would hide that pile of burgers.

So what's the big deal? We could take everything that outfit ever made right down to the last McNugget and hide it where nobody could find it. I wouldn't want to be the one to do the job, but just the thought of it calmed me down. It's a testimony to the size and ruggedness of our state that such an awesome entity as the world's largest fast-food empire could be digested by it whole, leaving not so much as a bad smell behind.

Alaska's people could take a lesson from her land. If a few hamburger stands are all it takes to break the spirit of Alaska, then we must have had a pretty precarious hold on it in the first place.

A Year of
Peace

During the Christmas season there was a banner alongside the road I drive home, bidding PEACE ON EARTH. I liked that. It was your typical holiday fare, but so much better than a mere "Merry Christmas" or "Noel" (I still can't figure out what that means).

Peace on Earth — as opposed to peace on the Moon or Pluto, I suppose — is a nice sentiment. I was a little disappointed when I noticed today the banner is gone, packed away in a garage or basement for safekeeping until the spirit of the season once again moves the owners to unfurl it. It's a shame there has to be a season for that sort of wish. I'd have thought none the less of them if they'd left it up.

Now that 1986 is history for everyone except tax accountants, I wonder if many of us remember much about it. All the "Year in Review" folderol in the media lately has done its best to remind us time and again of the *Challenger* disaster, upheaval in the Philippines, unrest in Central

America, and scandal in the White House. Natural disasters, technical failures, graft, disinformation, and weaponry seemed to dominate the headlines as they have every year in recent memory.

War toy sales reached historic highs in 1986. Not only at Toys-R-Us, but also in Congress, and in more than one unlikely country overseas. A strange statistic to emerge out of a year that was proclaimed the International Year of Peace by the United Nations. Maybe you didn't know it was. I don't think it made the "Best of '86" shows. Too many good train wrecks and too much bang-bang footage from Nicaragua to squeeze in a mention of something as uninteresting as peace, I suppose.

Of course not everyone neglected our token year of pacification. Several hundred individuals took it upon themselves to walk across the continent in the March for Peace. They arrived in Washington, D.C., eight and a half months later, triumphant, exuberant, exhausted, and ignored. Maybe you heard about this march. It made the news a few times. Like when it went bankrupt and the marchers had their porta-potties repossessed. Nice little humorous tidbit to round off the half hour before we went to sports and weather.

I recently read an account of this expedition, and the participants said they were mostly well received on their travels. They allowed as how the small-town folk of America would come out to greet them, wave, and cheer them on. Whether or not this was due to some philosophical alignment remains a mystery, but having lived all my life in small towns, I can testify that a herd of cattle going down Main Street would have elicited about the same response. It was the marchers' accounts of the negative reactions that really got to me. They made mention of the "one-finger peace sign" and the oft-repeated slogan "Peace Sucks."

Now, everything is a matter of taste, but of all the personally undesirable futures that might possibly lie before us, one of peace is certainly not among them. Even the last great man of war, General Douglas MacArthur, wrote in his memoirs that "no one prays for peace with as much earnest as does the soldier."

How anybody could have a problem with the idea of a peaceful world escapes me, but it might have something to do with conditioning. We've been trying to kill each other ever since we learned how to throw rocks. You don't get rid of that sort of behavior overnight. Rocks, having progressed to guided missiles, stealth bombers, and orbiting lasers, have rooted themselves firmly in our economy. War is everybody's bread and butter, and, by golly, don't you be messin' with my supper. I can't imagine why we came to be this way, and I'll be the first to admit it will take more than four hundred people on a walking tour of the country to undo it. As luck would have it, they were not the only ones with peace on their minds last year.

On a more local level, the Alaska Performing Artists for Peace cooked up a little cultural exchange with the Soviet Union. A very plausible idea, you must admit. If any Americans could find a common denominator with the Russians, it's us. We both live in really weird places. We share a hemisphere, a climate, a border, a native culture, and more than a couple of fish. If Alaskans can't get along with the Soviets, nobody can, and these folks went about trying to do just that.

Although most of the trip was funded out of their own pockets, one of our Homer participants told me a chilling tale of his efforts to raise local funding for the exchange. It seems that more than one fine and benevolent organization declined to donate because they thought the word "peace" in their title was "too political."

Gag me with a claymore, folks. The term "political" means to me that there are some opposing parties to a given idea. Communism is political. Capitalism is political. Who's gonna take out the garbage is political. But peace? C'mon. Is there a person on the face of this earth that hasn't stood up at one time or another and yelled, "Holy mackerel, what's a body gotta do to get some peace around here?"

What we gotta do is not easy to say, but until we figure it out, our desires might be best summed up by the words of one Yupik Eskimo. While on this Alaskan tour of the Soviet Union, the man had occasion to present a fur parka to a representative of Chairman Gorbachev's wife. His presentation speech went something like this:

"We of this small known segment of the universe deserve the very best, and the very best that we can give each other is peace."

I don't know how much this Yupik knows of politics, or if he even cares, but I trust Mrs. Gorbachev enjoyed her gift. God and bureaucracies willing, we'll have a few Russians over here next year bearing similar gifts. It might not do any good, but it sure as hell can't hurt anything.

"Peace on Earth." Wouldn't that be something to write home about? Maybe I'll go ask those folks with the roadside banner if I can put it back up for a while. I know I don't speak for everybody, but I hadn't grown tired of seeing it just yet.

Hard
Comparisons

I've never found it a healthy practice to compare myself to other people. It only leads to either smug satisfaction or abject self-pity, neither of which becomes me. I sometimes feel that other people are my competition — whether it be for money, smarts, popularity, or spiritual awareness — and even though it does no good, I continue to wage silent battle with my fellow travelers. I'd be a lot better off figuring out what makes me happy, and doing what I can to stay that way.

Of course this is easier said than done, and no matter how noble my intentions, I continue to hold myself up against other people whether I want to or not.

There are two times I've done this that stick out in my mind more than others. These two in particular stay with me because I won the contest I should have lost and lost the one that never should have been a challenge.

The contest I won took place in a swank hotel bar in Boston a year ago. I was on my maiden publicity tour, and the publisher of the book was treating me pretty good. There were a couple presidential visits commemorated in brass by the front door of this joint, and limos and Rolls-Royces were parked four deep on the street. I felt entirely out of my element, but decided to wallow in the good life just in case it never came around again.

While I was sitting in the bar one evening silently enjoying the fruits (or at least the hops) of success, a very drunk man broke me from my thoughts. I guessed him to be in his late thirties, and you didn't have to know a lot about clothes to see that his evening attire probably cost more than my truck did.

He was alone and trying to spark some conversation around the bar by talking too loud to nobody in particular. He claimed to be the heir to a huge corporate fortune and to own a controlling interest in a worldwide cosmetics company. He bragged that he inherited his pile at the tender age of eighteen, and moaned that everyone's been trying to take it from him ever since. He was closing up his Boston town house and building a "little ten-room" up at Kennebunkport, Maine, "to get away from it all." He wondered if you could get decent servants up in that wilderness.

The word "servants" raised my hackles, and I started to listen more closely. He hated his cars. His Rolls was always in the shop waiting for parts from "those damn Brits." He'd blown three transmissions in his Porsche in less than a year. The Mercedes "rode like a tank, and what's the use of driving one anyway now that all the pimps have them?"

He had to fly the SST to London in the morning and complained all the way out the door on unsteady legs how his "brains go right through the back of his head" when he rides that thing with a hangover.

I sat in my off-the-rack clothes nursing my cheap domestic beer and gloated. Even though my entire net worth wouldn't rotate the tires on his fleet of cars, I was the more fortunate man. He'd found more to complain about in a ten-minute tirade than I could come up with in a month.

I spent my last night in the good life with a different view of it. The next day I would fly coach back to Alaska, where I would be reunited with family, dear friends, and contentment, to name just three of the things that have obviously eluded that miserable soul at the bar. He had everything I should have envied, but all he got from me was pity. I won.

I would lose everything I won a year later in Seattle. Just a few weeks ago while on a similar tour, I had occasion to look out the window of another swank hotel. They were still treating me good, but I was getting a little tired of it. I had a cold and I missed my family. While pining away waiting for room service to bring me my version of a cold remedy, I spotted a man down on the street.

He was pushing a grocery cart of garbage bags full of God only knows what. He couldn't have been that old, but he carried himself like a *very* old man. It was obvious that everything he owned was in the cart. He had on three or four beat-up coats to ward off the Seattle rains, and my heart went out to him. But just as I was about to slip into pity he did the most incredible thing.

He pulled a rag out of his coat pocket and began polishing the public drinking fountain on the corner. "Some kind of nut," I thought. Then he pushed on and started cleaning up a parking meter. A few feet more and he was on a newspaper box. Every few wipes he would refold the rag to present a clean face and diligently go about his chore.

A store owner came out and started talking to him. I thought he was chasing him off, but it was soon apparent they were friends. The store owner gave him something. A few pedestrians walked by and greeted him as he went at his task. I was fascinated.

Here was a man who had lost everything, or maybe never had it. He had every reason to lie under a trestle somewhere and drink bad wine until it all went away, but he didn't. He worked his way up the street making friends and doing some small thing for the privilege of being there.

I was beaten hands down. There I sat in a room that cost more money than he'll see in a year, and I was depressed. Had he ventured a look into my window, he'd have seen a long face in a fancy chair. He might have felt sorry for me. Sorry that I was alone in a strange city without the benefit of all the good people he knew. He won.

I guess you could call this contest even, but I'm not so sure. All the standard lessons are there. Every luxury in the world can't buy happiness, and all the hard times won't necessarily break it. There's no good reason to be intimidated by anyone as we go through these little comparisons with each other. You win some, you lose some. It's best not to play the game at all. Especially in this little world we live in, a world in which anything can happen. Like these two guys of mine could turn out to be one and the same person.

Now, *that* would be intimidating.

NOT LETTING GO

———— ❖ ————

Eulogy for
an Ancient Eskimo

O ne of the deepest fears we all share is that of dying
alone and without recognition. Not recognition in
the sense of a *New York Times* obituary or a national mon-
ument, but just a simple acknowledgment that we've
passed. Something in the deepest part of our being requires
that our life mean something to others. For our death to go
unnoticed and unrecorded would be virtually to deny that
we were ever here at all.

We humans have always had our share of problems,
but by far the biggest one is our tendency to wear out, drop
dead, and rot away without a trace. Since we've yet to figure
out how to keep from dropping dead, we've devoted a lot
of time over the centuries to figuring out better ways to
leave traces of ourselves.

Scientists are still poking around the pyramids in
Egypt trying to decipher all that's there. Probably the fan-
ciest tombstones ever built, these crypts of kings are the

prime example of our desire to be remembered. From records of their daily lives to the treasures they decided to take along with them to the afterlife, these things served to defy the pharaoh's own mortality and say to future generations, "See how I was."

Our culture is lucky this way. We know a lot about how we used to be because of our determination to be remembered. Down through the millennia, men and women great and small have chronicled their deeds for us to study. Three thousand years after his passing, the Boy King Tut lives in the books of schoolchildren and historians. Simple fishermen from biblical times have their names repeated from pulpits and pews, classrooms and kitchens the world over. We have our Michelangelos and Martin Luthers, our painters and popes, saints and scientists, every one of them destined to live on in the minds of their descendants for as long as their descendants have minds.

Somewhere about the time one of these lucky ducks, Galileo, was dropping things off a tippy tower in Pisa trying to get a handle on gravity, a lesser-known man was trying to get a handle on the weather in another part of the world — Utqiagvik, "Place Where We Hunt Snowy Owls." It would one day be known as Barrow, Alaska, "Place Where a Pizza Costs Close to Fifty Bucks," but that wouldn't be for another four hundred years or so.

In the meantime there were more important things for this guy to worry about. There was one helluva storm brewing out over the Arctic Ocean, and he didn't like the looks of it. He'd heard the elders' stories of the dreaded *ivu,* winds that would send the loose pack ice bulldozing onto land at blinding speeds. His house was dug into the frost perilously close to the beach. He paced the bluff listening to his mukluks scuff the fall tundra and worried. Should he head inland until this all blew over? No, he needed to stay here for the seal hunting when the sea finally froze.

He looked forward to the winter, to being tucked away safely in his house of driftwood and sod. The dim glow of the burning seal oil would light the faces of his visitors, fellow hunters with their tales of bravado. Recounting the bounty of the whale harvest. Sharing their strategies for tracking the caribou. Speaking quietly of ancient times and strange things. The *ivu*.

No, he would stay. He returned to his house, out of the wind, and lay on his bed of baleen. Watching the shadows of the seal oil lamp play on the walls, he daydreamed to get his mind off the sound of the pack ice scraping and cracking outside. He recalled the hunt that landed the bowhead whale whose parts he now rested on. He fingered the bags of food tied to his waist and his fine shirt. He was a lucky man. He drifted off to dream of his father, and *his* father. He slept and dreamed of children, and their children, and theirs. How they would know of him and what a fine and fortunate man he was.

A terrible noise rose out of the sea and woke him. He grabbed at the shaft of his harpoon in reflex, but there was no enemy to fight, only tons of ice crashing down through his house and onto him. It was over. Death had come.

Our fortunate Eskimo had just joined the ranks of the Boy King and Julius Caesar, with one exception: he left no mark. The ocean's gravel covered him, and it's possible not a soul who knew him ever learned what became of the man. Nothing of him remained for the children to know, or theirs to teach. He realized the deepest fear of all mankind, to die alone and unknown.

Some four hundred years would pass. The "Place Where We Hunt Snowy Owls" became the place where white men hunted lots of whales. They brought with them their ways, their religion, and their names. Utqiagvik is now a city of 3,000 Americans and the descendants of our lost Eskimo are driving cars made in Detroit. They live in modern homes with sheetrock walls and pay a lot for a pizza.

He might have liked pizza, most people do, but that's not important. What's important is what he *did* like, what he didn't like, and just exactly what he was. It's important to his heirs, who live their lives precariously on the edge of America and the twentieth century, who cling desperately to the heritage that produced them.

The need to know is powerful. The need to be known is at least as great. The two together can do incredible things.

Just such a thing happened not too long ago in Barrow. A powerful fall storm, much like the one that killed this man, washed huge chunks of earth into the sea. A modern Eskimo village was being threatened. A modern Eskimo paced the bluffs listening to his mukluks scuff the fall tundra. He worried and watched, and while he was watching he spotted something.

A single frozen mukluk-clad leg was sticking out from a gravel bank. An ancient Eskimo, harpoon at his side and bags of food tied to his waist, lay on a bed of baleen. As the storm raged on, specialists were called in. Archaeologists, reporters, photographers. Work began to protect this incredible find. There would be no way to study it now until spring. Money would be needed. Heavy equipment.

Modern shelter. Barricades the best minds of our day could muster would be erected.

But there are many powers in this world greater than the wants of men. The storm wound up to a force that hadn't been seen in years. Although the *ivu* never came, there was enough damage done without it. When things settled down, the current residents of Utqiagvik tallied their losses.

Apartment buildings and houses teetered on the ocean's edge. Roads were washed away, the waterfront a shambles. Disaster aid from a governmental system inconceivable to the mind of our good man poured in to repair the damage. But there was a loss that will never be recovered. Our man was gone. Washed clean of this earth, and despite the greatest efforts of men, passed on to the ages.

Scientists would mourn him for the information lost about an era of great mystery. His descendants would mourn the opportunity to learn of themselves and honor him with burial in a faith they now hold dear. A writer who knows little of science or Eskimos would see a picture of his leg on the back page of a newspaper. It would cause him to wonder about such things as death, posterity, and the lives of ordinary men and women.

There the man lay in black and white. Arrows on the page pointed out his "toe" and "heel." The toe was pointed down. The caption made note of the baleen bed, harpoon, and food bags. The writer's imagination got the better of him, and he befriended this old Eskimo with a foot in two centuries. The writer consoled himself as he thought many times, "Rest easy, old friend. Your passing has not gone without notice."

Ohlsen Mountain

It was about a year ago that workers removed the dish antenna from the Ohlsen Mountain radar site. The Ohlsen Mountain facility was part of the old Defense Early Warning System which the military set up to watch for incoming ballistic missiles. The whole system was made obsolete and abandoned years ago, but the antenna and some old buildings still stand atop the naturally flat-topped mountain.

Our front window looks out on Ohlsen Mountain. It's a few miles away, and not the most arresting feature in our view, but it's right smack dab in the middle of it all the same. I didn't think that antenna bothered me, and never realized it did until they took it down. It was only today I gave it any real thought at all.

When we look out our windows, we see some pretty well-put-together hills. Right below us sits an old red barn with a metal roof and fading paint. If I knew it only from a photograph, I'd have placed it in the New England countryside. Over and beyond the green hills, including Ohlsen Mountain, stand the white granite peaks and glaciers of the Kenai Mountain Range. There are better views of the world to be had, but probably not much better.

During our long summer evenings, it's nice to sit in the window and admire the landscape. As the sun sets behind us, the shadow of twilight makes its way up the green hills until just the very tops are all that's left of the day.

That's when that antenna would really come into focus. Because it was made out of metal, the sun would spotlight it. Being the tallest point of land in our vicinity, it was always the last thing to go dark. Long after the red barn was buried in shadow and the spruce groves and alder patches were lost to the dusk, there'd be this lone radar dish, gleaming in self-importance. It was the last thing I saw before I looked away and went to bed. It pointed straight up in the sky but wasn't aimed at anything anymore, having been relieved of duty by better watchdogs in outer space or someplace. Still, it was an effective reminder of the dangerous world we live in, like a nervous gunfighter watching his back in a crowded room.

It couldn't have done anything to stop a missile, but it could see one coming. Give maybe twenty minutes' notice to Omaha or Dubuque. Time enough for prayers and curses. Time enough for our guys to shoot back. These were the kinds of thoughts I used to take to bed with me.

I guess it was only last night I realized I was sitting in the window longer than I used to. I noticed that the white peaks across the bay are now the last things to go dark. They turn a pale rose color, and sometimes, if the angle of the sun is just right, some of the glaciers take on a power of their own, as if the ice itself were on fire. Sort of poetic, but not being a poet, I'm not sure what to do with the experience. It's fine with me just to sit and admire it.

They say that body of land over there hails from South America, that it drifted up here millions of years ago and married itself to the North Pacific plate. The collision pushed those mountains up in the air where it's cold enough to hold glaciers that reflect bright light into the window where I sit. These are the kind of thoughts I take to bed with me these days, big thoughts spanning millions of years of history and holding out the implied promise of a million more to come.

Seems like I'm sleeping better this summer, but I might be imagining it. I can't say if the last thing a person sees before he hits the hay has anything to do with the way he sleeps; all I can say is I'm glad they finally took the antenna off the top of Ohlsen Mountain.

State of Spring

Springtime in Alaska is more a state of mind than it is a state of affairs. The days do get longer, but only so we can watch it snow all the way into evening. There are no sure signs that summer's on the way.

Spring is supposed to be a period of grace, a sort of mental pause in which to gather our wits about us after a long, hard winter. Alaskans are robbed of that. By the time it feels like spring it's already summer, and time to go out and be somebody again. It's like being sent off to work without our morning coffee. There are no spring songbirds out my bedroom window bidding me to come alive. Just the sounds of a neighbor rocking his car out of a frost boil.

Real hints of spring are hard to come by. The only signs I've seen for sure are the ones the highway department put up to tell us our studded tires are now illegal. I love those signs. When studs are outlawed, only outlaws have studs, and I like the image. I pull on the ol' Levi's jacket, snap my chewing gum, and speed down the dry pavement savoring the criminal whine of metal on asphalt. It ain't exactly the Sundance Kid, but not bad for a married guy.

Other spring indicators try to get my attention, like the genetic curse that triggers me to clean things. Once our yard glacier recedes, I while away the hours picking things out of the mud. I sort it into two piles: my stuff and somebody else's stuff.

I don't know how or why junk migrates in the winter, but it does. Exotic garbage turns up in my yard. Campaign posters, yogurt cups, and chrome parts of unfamiliar cars sneak onto my domain under the cover of snow, while some of my own stuff defects.

A fairly new double-bit ax left out in a December snowstorm has mysteriously slipped away. I suspect it eloped with the cap to my propane tank, or the extension cord I used for the Christmas lights. I wish them nothing but the best. I pile the muddy things I recognize as mine next to the garage, to be ignored at a later date. Other junk is heaped in the back of the truck, and when it's full I lose interest in cleaning anything.

The truck sits in the pool of pudding my wife and I use as a driveway. I suppose that's another sign of spring I've failed to mention. Our perennial bog returns, a boot-sucking mass of sinister mud that presently has my truck in its slimy grip. What's the use of tidying up? It's like washing windows while the living room rug is on fire. Nothing is going to look good with that going on, so I quit and sulk for a while.

It just isn't fair. Other places get springs full of cherry blossoms and tulips. The air turns sweet, and people turn frisky. All we ever get is a mess to clean up.

I remember the springs of my youth, when I had no trouble getting into the swing of the season. My adolescent sap rose to fever levels. The school year tapered down to a matter of weeks when misdirected energies could be applied to any number of ill-conceived notions. A whole new summer lay ahead to be spent a year older than the one before. Added privileges, maybe even a job. God help me, maybe even a *car*. It was too much to handle. I'd sit in algebra class staring past the green maples into a new era. Teachers tried in vain to hold my attention while my knees bounced and my feet worked the pedals of an imaginary GTO. I was immune to their efforts. They had no idea they were competing with destiny.

Some destiny this turned out to be, slogging around in an unkempt yard, kicking absently at the frozen earth and cussing a truck that couldn't hold a candle to my dream wheels of yesteryear. It's filthy and stuck and full of vile things that have to be taken to the dump, and I can't stand the sight of it. It makes me tired and I go sit down behind the garage.

There is this one spot on the south side of the garage that's always warm. The sandy ground is bare and dry, and the cool breeze doesn't find its way back there. It's a good place to sit. That's where the dog is, and dogs always know the best places to lie around.

It gets kind of hot when the sun comes out and feels good to open the coat and pull a few buttons. Sun on bare skin, not too bad. If I close my eyes I can be almost anywhere at any time, even on my folks' back stoop with the smell of freshly turned earth from gardens and farms on the wind. Not bad at all.

You know, with a couple more days of this, the sun might dry that muck right up. As soon as the frost is out of the ground, a guy will be able to dig in it. Maybe I'll put in that barbecue pit we've talked about every year. Have some friends out for steaks and volleyball, or just sit around and smack gnats. We could have a real nice place here if we fixed the yard up a little. I should put that fence up, too. Wouldn't that set the place off?

I start working an imaginary post-hole digger with one foot, while counting off how many posts it will take with the other. I could haul some slab wood from the mill for the rails. Probably get all of it in one load as soon as I get that junk out of the truck. Good a day as any for a drive if I can get it free of the mud.

Put on the ol' Levi's jacket and take the dog for a ride. Go to the dump. Check out the mill. By God, I think I'll even run that old truck through the car wash while I'm in town. What the heck. It's spring.

Back to School

He couldn't have weighed much more than his new raincoat. It was so new, in fact, that it wouldn't let his arms hang the way they should. They stuck out from his sides at an odd angle, and he could no more scratch his nose than he could turn his head strapped into the hood. He stood stiffly beside the road and watched me coming from a long way. As I passed him he looked at me with his lip curled under his front teeth in fear.

When I found him again in my rear-view mirror, I saw it wasn't me he'd been looking at at all, but the big yellow school bus behind me. "Oh, that's right," I thought. "First day of school." I wanted to turn around and go comfort him, but was called off by something remembered in his expression. Yes, the kid was scared, but his eyes were fixed on the bus with such defiance that I knew he didn't need any counsel. He was going through with it. Brave as any soldier, he was going to get on that bus for the very first time. I drove on while a similar bus in a similar rain charged out of my memory in fourth gear.

I hadn't been to kindergarten. That's what had me worried. I knew my colors and I could count past a hundred, but I couldn't spell at all. My mother assured me I didn't need to spell to go to first grade. That's what they wanted to teach me. But I wasn't so sure. My older brother was way up in the third grade, and he could spell like crazy. He had me convinced I was a mental defective and the nuns at our small parochial school would serve me for hot lunch the first day if I didn't get my act together.

Determined to measure up, I asked my brother what it took to spell. "Lots of paper and some pencils," he said. The pencils were covered. I'd already sharpened the life out of all three fat number ones in my Roy Rogers pencil box, and their big pink erasers were good and broken in. It was the paper that had me worried. Mom had told me the school would give me what I needed, but I couldn't trust her. She wasn't going to school, and my brother, who was, had explicitly mentioned paper. So I stole the whole stack of typing paper from the kitchen drawer and slipped it under my brand-new yellow raincoat.

Standing by the mailboxes with my brother, I was probably as scared as I ever have been since. Six years old and functionally illiterate. Buckled into an impossible raincoat I wasn't sure I could find my way out of without maternal assistance. The only thing I had going for me was a Roy Rogers pencil box, a Davy Crockett lunch pail, and over four hundred sheets of stolen typing paper. The hardest thing I ever did in my life was step onto that bus.

I'd like to be able to say that all my worrying was for naught, but it wasn't. Actually, as I reached this mythical place called Saint Sebastian's Elementary, my worst fears were realized.

Upon approaching the first-grade classroom I was greeted by Sister Antonio. I'd never been so close to a nun before and wasn't sure just how to act. When she smiled and said, "Good morning," it was as if a burning bush had spoken. Until that moment I had never heard a nun speak. My only experience of them had been watching them in church in their mysterious black-and-white robes. I had some twisted notion that they were all related to Saint Peter — a good friend of Jesus' — and none of these people were to be taken lightly. I nearly swallowed my tongue as I stumbled past her into the room. That's where the real trouble started.

All the desks were in neat rows, and each one had a little folded card on top. "Find the desk with your name on it and take your seat, Tommy," I heard her say from the door. Other kids I'd never seen before were gracefully finding their places and admiring their name cards. I didn't even know what my name looked like. I stalled around the aisles until there were only two empty seats. Taking my best shot, I marched up, plopped down my Davy Crockett lunch pail, and collapsed with relief into Tammy Beech's chair.

The details are fuzzy from there, but I think I was found out during roll call. I vaguely remember Sister Antonio looming over my desk and saying something like, "You don't even know your own name?" This was the last thing I needed pointed out in the presence of my very first peer group. Still in my raincoat, I clumsily got out of my chair and dislodged the four hundred–odd sheets of paper that were precariously stashed underneath. They cascaded across the floor in an impressive display and proceeded to soak up the mud and water left by thirty first-graders. First-graders being how they are about wiping their feet, it's a good thing I brought as much paper as I did.

To say I could've died would be an understatement. I blushed so hard my ears rang. The thing I remember most about picking up that paper was the presence of the burning bush right behind me in eternal silence, the cruel giggles of my classmates, and the pounding of my broken little heart.

Of course, I lived through all this and went on to finish my first year of school. I got used to Sister Antonio and, believe it or not, she even taught me how to spell. I was never served up for hot lunch, and I played Joseph in the Christmas play.

All these memories came back to me when I passed that little guy on the road. All the fear and uncertainty that come with a strange new land. All the pain and humiliation that go with screwing it up. And everything we learn in the process. It never stops, and it never seems to get any easier.

I must say, though, how encouraged I was by that small face along the road. Biting his lip in terror, but with pure resolve in his eye, he reminded me all over again of the best lesson I ever learned. If you want to go somewhere, you gotta get on the bus.

Last
Dollar

I've been at different stages of being broke all my life. My last dollar has slipped through my fingers more times than I care to remember.

The first last dollar I ever spent was earned on a paper route. Every morning I would diligently teeter out of the driveway on a wreck of a bicycle and deliver the morning news. It was a dismal occupation even on its best days, but it provided me with the first real money I ever had. What a heavenly feeling to march into the bank and open a savings account with a whole five dollars. Five turned to ten and ten to twenty, until pretty soon I felt the riches of the world lay at my feet. My parents advised me that what money I made was mine to do with as I pleased.

It didn't take me too long to fix on something I wanted. As bicycles were a big part of my life at the time, a replacement for my wreck was the obvious choice. I recruited new subscribers on my route to spur things along, and as the route got bigger, the size of the bike I needed increased in direct proportion. About the time my route grew to such a size that nothing short of Mom and the family station wagon could get me through it before school, I reached the magic number.

Taking my entire wad into Three Rivers Schwinn, I walked the familiar path to that big black beauty in the window. Mustering all the self-importance that ninety-five self-made dollars could confer on a ten-year-old boy, I told the manager my intentions. I had him fit it up front with a two-bushel basket. I commissioned him to install a generator light, handlebar hooks, and side carriers, and even got a rear-view mirror with the change. I walked out of that store the best-outfitted paper carrier in three states.

I had everything I wanted in the world. For a time things went along smoothly. Then one dim morning, while I was loading papers onto my customized truck of a bicycle, it dawned on me. I *did* have everything I wanted in this world. Suddenly, and without provocation, I lost my will to work. Why go on aimlessly earning when I sat astride all the happiness money could buy? My paper route became the first victim of a character flaw that would mold my life for many years to come. It didn't take long for my last dollar to go, but I still had my bike, and life was good.

They say all things must pass, and this one certainly did. As childhood made its wary way into adolescence, my interests grew beyond black bicycles with half-ton payloads. Certain members of the opposite sex began attracting my attention. Although I wasn't exactly sure what it was, I was certain everything I wanted in life somehow involved them. Of course the operating costs of pursuing this enigma soon found me flipping hamburgers for ninety cents an hour. I spent my last dollar every Saturday night during this period, but life was good again and getting more promising by the day.

A hot grill soon gave way to a dime-store stockroom when I decided that true inner peace could only be reached with a new stereo. Not long after my last dime-store dollar was handed over to the Sony Corporation, the frustration of being a biped in a four-wheeled society snatched happiness from my grasp once again.

After a long, hot summer in a furnace factory, I found myself content behind the wheel of a '55 Pontiac Star Chief that smelled of chickens, and on my way to college. The last dollar from a night job as a janitor went toward a fine new guitar, and life became good once again. What with poverty being somewhat of a badge of honor on college campuses, it remained good for a very long time.

I don't know exactly when it happened, but sometime after entering the real work force I stopped earning for contentment and just started earning. Money no longer represented particular fancies. It became a necessity. Last dollars turned into a serious and dangerous thing.

There was no paying for the groceries and rent and taking the rest of the year off. Vehicles broke down at the worst possible times and had to be replaced with less than the stuff of dreams. New furniture, real estate, and tropical vacations were sometimes realized, but more often foiled by every conceivable expense between income tax and illness.

After marrying each other, my wife and I discovered the principle of buy now, pay later. We sold our souls to a thirty-year mortgage and a succession of car payments with matching insurance policies. All our disposable income is calculated a year in advance and spent the year before. Our last dollar shows itself every thirty days and will continue to appear on schedule for as far ahead as we can see.

Sometimes I wonder what we're really working for, and I sit in the living room to brood. There must be some comfort in this.

The wood in the stove shifts and I'm grateful for the heat. The phone rings bringing news from family and I'm glad we can accept the charges. My wife pulls into the driveway in a car that's at least half ours, carrying groceries that are all ours. A ten-dollar refund came from Sears so she bought a bottle of wine. Sitting upstairs, we watch the moon rise over the mountains and talk about our day. Amusing stories replace problems, and we decide we love our jobs. The wine makes us sleepy, and while leaning against a not-so-fancy couch there isn't much left to say.

Not much, that is, but what I've always said: life is good to me. Like it always has been. Every last dollar of it.

Pretty As
a Picture

I've been told that I take lousy pictures. It's not that my shots aren't technically okay, it's just that my pictures seem to bring out the worst in people. I hope that's not a sign of something. If looking through another person's eyes would be a good way of finding out how he sees the world, you'd think that looking through his camera would be the next best thing. Well, I think very highly of people; in fact, some of my best friends are people. So why are all the pictures I have of my friends ugly?

Other people's pictures have folks in them with a lot of white teeth. They're looking right at you with big, smiles and flattering character lines etched across their faces. Maybe they're smelling a fresh flower with eyes half closed in thoughtful appreciation, or toasting you with a drink at a long-gone celebration of some momentous sort or another.

My pictures will capture people in conversation, which is a big mistake. You can video-tape a conversation, but you can't take a snapshot of it. People's mouths make really funny shapes when they're talking, and if you shoot a person saying even a good word like "wonderful," you'll freeze their lips in some oddball position like a monkey's. I'm famous for doing that, and people who know me don't like me hanging around with a camera.

I take a lot of candid pictures at parties and picnics. Those can really get you into trouble at a slide show. I always manage to capture some poor guy glancing at the rear end of the wrong woman. Of course almost every man does this at one time or another, but even an innocent look, when caught on film, can become eternal lechery. I usually end up throwing away half the pictures I take. It's not that they're deceiving. They're just too honest.

It's true what they say about a camera never lying, but you certainly can lie to a camera. We do it all the time. At least we exaggerate things a little. The first thing you'll hear when you point a lens at someone is, "Wait, I'm not ready." So you wait while your subject brushes the crumbs off his chin, puts out a cigarette, or throws an arm around the person next to him like they've been standing that way all day. You get your picture, but it's blown all out of proportion. Everybody's having a little more fun than they really were, and liking each other more than they actually do.

We've all been guilty of putting on a show for the camera at one time or another. You're with your sweetheart traveling somewhere. You've been walking and complaining about the price of the room, the blister on your heel, and the rude waitress at the café. Then you stop somebody on the street, hand them your Kodak, and put on your very best "having a wonderful time" smile. Ten years later you'll look at that picture in a scrapbook and remember what a great trip it was, whether it was or not. It's a worthy thing to do, plant these little seeds of contentment in our lives should we someday doubt we ever had any.

It's good practice to take these opportunities to mug up to a camera. There never seems to be one around for the real special times. That make-up embrace after a long and dangerous discussion. The look on your face as you hold the phone and hear that you got the job. The quiet ride home from the hospital after learning that suspicious lump was benign, only something to watch but not to worry about. Those are the moments that should be preserved, to be remembered and relied upon when harder times take hold. Those times when a photographer like me will catch you at a party with a loneliness on your face that you didn't think would show. Or bitterness tugging at your lips during a conversation you didn't intend to be overheard.

We all slip up like this sometimes, and sooner or later we get caught with our guard down. I think that's why I end up with pictures like I do. I like it when people leave their guard down. We all know our best side, and it's nice to keep that faced forward whenever we can. But I don't mind having pictures of the other sides. My collection of faces may not be as attractive as other photographers' albums, but they're my friends, and they all look just like people to me.

Working
Slobs

Not everybody can put his finger on the single dumbest thing he ever did, but I can. I barely got away with my life. I was twenty-one, and I'd just been hired on by a cannery to help build a new four-story steel building. It was winter, all the iron was covered with snow and ice, and the foreman needed another squirrely little guy to work the high beams and bolt the roof members together.

"You afraid of heights?" was all the foreman wanted to know. "No," was all I had to answer. Needless to say that was not entirely true, but at the moment I was more scared of not getting the job than I was of high places. He strapped a leather tool bag to me that held about ten pounds of wrenches and another ten pounds of nuts and bolts. "Have at it," he said, and pointed to an overextended aluminum ladder that reached almost to the top of the framework. The fact that it only *almost* reached the top is significant because that's what prompted me to attempt a stunt that I've yet to match in the way of bonehead maneuvers.

When I climbed to the end of this ladder — a broken-down old thing that would have made any OSHA inspector gag on his citation book — I realized I couldn't reach the top of the beam I was supposed to go to work on. Fully stretched out on the last rung, I was still a good six inches short of my objective and, undoubtedly, my job. So, wielding all the common sense a young man in dire need of work could muster, I jumped.

Like I say, I got away with it. My mittened hands made the edge of the iron to the first knuckle and I was able to monkey my way onto it. It was a lucky break. If the fall hadn't killed me, a rusty re-bar sticking up out of the snow on a twelve-inch center would have. What people throughout history have laid on the line for God and country, I'd risked for six-fifty an hour.

I can never recall that incident without a wave of anxiety overtaking me. I see my own young face frozen in astonishment. A broken body impaled on nine dollars' worth of steel reinforcement. Four dollars' worth of nuts and bolts and a few worn wrenches scattered around me. We've all done things in our life we'd handle differently if given another chance, and this might be one of mine.

If I was on that same ladder today I wouldn't jump. I'd climb down and tell the foreman he needed a longer ladder. Or more likely, I'd complain about the safety of the whole operation and demand a job on the ground. That would be the smart thing to do, but sometimes there are greater rewards than being just another smart guy. Like hugging a piece of frosted steel with your eyes closed until your heart calms down enough to sit up. Like having the veteran iron-worker on the next beam shake his head with an admiring grin and say, "So they sent a wildman to help me, eh?" Being invited into the old-timers' circle on the first day of the job and listening to your veteran partner recount your deed to an appreciative coffee shack audience. Overhearing your foreman explaining to the contractor that the new guy is shaping up fine. "He's a good worker": the highest honor that can be bestowed on a working slob. Yeah, I wouldn't have the guts to try it again, but I think I'd want to.

I'm not sure why all of this has come to mind just now. Maybe it's because I'm not working this year. Oh, I'm working, I guess, if you can call poking at letters on a plastic keyboard "work." I'm not convinced that it is yet. After spending all of my adult life trying to be a "good worker," I feel like I'm sloughing off.

All my friends are workers. They come by the house sometimes with concrete on their pants and Band-Aids on their fingers. I offer them beers, and their first three gulps are big and thirsty. I don't get very thirsty anymore, and my hands are healed and pink. For the first time in ten years the cuticles have actually attached themselves to my finger-nails. I can't remember them ever being that way, and they look strange. I can open my hands up all the way and it doesn't hurt. You wouldn't think a person could miss a thing like pain, but I remember that ache with some fond-ness. That feeling when you lie down in bed after eight hours of finishing concrete. Your knees untie themselves and your shoulders melt into the pillow. I miss the morning shower bringing to life the cuts and scratches from the day before. I don't know, I guess it was such a *worthy* feeling.

And I miss the company. I work alone now, and the few people I need to talk to for my writing are smart, careful people. They think about what they're saying and try not to offend. They are not the kind of people who would lunge for slippery beams from an overextended ladder, or appreciate anyone else who pulls stunts like that. I don't talk about that stuff much anymore, but I think about it.

I think about it when I pass a construction site. I hear the *patunk-patunk* of an air nailer and remember what it was like when a good crew got on a head of steam to finish a job. Skilled people plying their trade, taking a chance, making a buck. The crude jokes as thick and annoying as the rattle of the air compressor. Leaning on pickup trucks at the end of the day with a few atta-boys. Maybe piling into a tavern for a quick and spirited beer that would shame anything Miller ever put in a TV commercial.

And I think about it when I hear about a guy blown away when the steel beam he was guiding touched a high power line. Or a friend who stepped into the blind spot of a dump truck and got his legs broken. I remember how dangerous it is and what working people put up with to make a living. Mostly I remember the pride that came with being that way.

It might all be looking better to me in hindsight, or these pretty pink hands of mine could finally be getting on my nerves. Whatever it is, I feel this ache sometimes. It's not the ache that comes of hard work, though. I think it's the ache to work hard again.

Orphans

I am constantly amazed at the way things happen. Unexplainable coincidences occur that add an air of mystery to an otherwise predictable world. The very best of these leave positive evidence of a supreme and playful Being. I've always denied being superstitious, but these occasions of the uncanny make me want to reconsider. I look at them as omens, and like as not, I live my life by them.

There was a time a dozen years ago when I sat in a dorm room at a Michigan college and felt the flatlands of the Midwest closing around my neck. I had to get out of there. The drudgery of school was driving me nuts, and I was tired of leading a life that could be summed up in twenty-five words or less. I needed to *do* something.

I had a good friend I hadn't seen in a couple of years. His family had moved to another state, and he too was pursuing an uneventful student career. In high school we had dreamed together of thumbing rides into the sunset —

Colorado, California, the Great Northwest, and on our best days, Alaska, the spiritual mecca of all would-be adventurers.

I went to the phone to call him. I wanted to talk him into bagging college and heading out on a lark with me. When I picked up the receiver there was no dial tone. I rattled the button and finally heard a "Hello?" It was my friend. He'd called me for the first time in six months while I was about to call him for the first time in a year. What was on his mind made it even sweeter. He was ready to go, and did I want to come along?

Needless to say, I never looked back. Any doubts I might have had about sacrificing my education, disappointing my parents, or ruining my life dissolved with that one divine coincidence.

It turned out to be a good trip. Many omens and adventures later find me living in my mecca and pursuing the career I was training for at college in the first place. So nothing was sacrificed after all. My friend and I separated early in the journey, but he ended up here too. He lives in Healy and does surveying for the coal company, also his field of study in that other life.

This is just one example of some of the markers I've used to map the path I walk on. You can see how, after a few of these timely twists of fate, I might come to rely on them. They tend to hold things together for me. Sort of a reassurance that I am indeed still on the trail. Each is a blaze on a random trunk in a forest full of trees.

The reason I'm bringing all this up is that I've just wandered across another one of these blazes. Today I received a postcard from a well-known artist in Seward. She just wanted to drop me a line to compliment me on something she'd read. Flattered, I returned the favor with a bit of raving on a painting I'd seen of hers.

It was of the Jesse Lee Hayes Home in Seward, an old orphanage. It was abandoned, I believe after the '64 quake, and duly gutted sometime later. It stands now as a haunting memorial to displaced and lonely children, many of them innocent victims of a rapidly evolving frontier. In the painting she had depicted the spirits of these children boiling from the empty entrance of the orphanage and sweeping into the sky. I'm not a great connoisseur of art, and I don't know if it's even one of her better works, but it left a big impression on me.

You see, I used to live there. It was the first place I ever called home here in Alaska. A bunch of us were working at the cannery in Seward, and the old orphanage was our unofficial bunkhouse that summer. There were maybe ten of us there at any one time. All just a couple years out of the house, we took to calling ourselves "the orphans." We were young men with no discernible futures or aspirations, and we'd sit around candles late at night singing songs and talking fish. It was a wonderful summer.

I never knew what happened to all the other orphans. Some returned to schools, I suppose. Others headed off to see more distant lands. One, I understand, is a writer in New Hampshire, and another is still with the canneries, now in Southeast Alaska. The rest I know nothing about other than first names.

I haven't dwelled on it a lot over the years, but as wonderful summers are apt to do, that season in Seward comes to mind from time to time. That's when I'll think of all the orphans and what's become of us.

I went through this when I first saw the painting, and again today as I wrote to the artist about it. It struck me as I redescribed her work to her how much like her spirit children we more fortunate orphans were. All young and without real direction, we burst from our summer friendships with the same energy and reckless abandon.

That's more poetic than I like to be, but there's a purpose to all this. While I lingered once again around that wonderful summer, the phone rang. It was another of those incredible coincidences. On the line was Paul, one of my orphans. He was in the area and just had a thought to get ahold of me after ten years for old times' sake. Call me a liar if you want, but I have witnesses.

He came by the house, we had a beer, talked some fish, exchanged addresses, and that's about the size of it. Paul was retiring his commercial fishing career and heading to California to pursue something less risky, but nothing in particular. We marveled a little at where we'd each ended up, and promised to stay in touch. Maybe we will. You know how those things go. Somebody moves and forgets to tell you. More important people and things get in the way, and pretty soon you become a misfiled card in an old friend's Rolodex. It's nothing personal. Nobody can ever guess what the future might bring.

I gave up guessing a long time ago. I don't mind not knowing where I'm headed. As long as these little blazes keep reassuring me that I'm still on the trail.

Nice to see you, Paul.

WOW

Among the thousand and one truisms that were hurled at us as expectant parents was one I especially wanted to believe: "You are going to learn the most important things from your children." It sounded so promising, and when accompanied by a smug veteran-parent grin, it appeared to hold water.

I looked forward to learning about these "most important things," but soon after our boy arrived I decided it was all a lot of tripe. If the most important things are pricing Pampers, holding tempers, and coming up with six-hundred variations on the word "no," then I figured people's ideas of "important" are purely subjective.

My partner in crime and I have spent the last twenty months with our child teaching him everything from rolling over to the dynamics of liquids in cups not carefully handled. All the while I held on to the hope that one day the teaching would leave off and the learning begin. Apparently it was just a matter of time, and the time, at last, has arrived.

We recently had occasion, as a family, to spend the night at the house of some friends in town. They have an extra room down in the basement, and we were set up with the bed and crib in the same room. No big deal. The kids went to sleep early, we had wonderful late-night conversation, and retired to our accommodations. I slept well but woke up too early, realized I was in a strange place, and couldn't go back to sleep.

In our natural habitat my wife and I don't share a room with the baby. We normally first come to know he's awake by a series of screams from downstairs that would put any self-respecting banshee to shame. But lying there wide awake in an unfamiliar house offered me the opportunity to hear my child wake up for the first time. This is where the learning came in.

Let me establish here that there are only a few words in our boy's vocabulary. "More" is the one we hear most often and can refer to anything from fun to food. "No" comes in a close second as he repeats it just about as often as he hears it. "Hello," "Bye-bye," "Momma," and "Daddy" make up the rest of his standard casual conversation, and that's all the words he's got. All, that is, but one.

By far his most distinguished and seldom-used expression is the word "wow." He only says "wow" when something really impresses him. If Dad lets a frying pan catch on fire and juggles it out the front door into the snow, it's "wow." If we turn around backwards on the way to town and hit the ditch at thirty, it's "wow." If the house were to burn down around him with the Messiah whispering reassurances into his ear the whole time, I'm confident he would sum it all up with "wow."

My reason for going into all this is, like I said, I had

occasion to hear him come to life one recent morning. I'd been awake for over an hour, but nobody else was up. I lay there silently straining to hear any encouraging sign that there might be people and coffee about. I thought about my day, a Sunday, and took inventory of the chores at hand. We would have to get organized and make the drive home. Once there I'd have wood to put up, a door to fix, a few letters to write, and some bills to pay. My wife would clean the house, as she does every Sunday. The boy would refuse to take a nap, as *he* does every Sunday. Luck willing, we would have a little time to spend together before Monday once again descended on our lives. All this was less than the stuff of dreams.

As I was lying there brooding, I heard my child stir. He rolled over — I assume he opened his eyes — and said "wow." Suddenly, I felt like a heel.

With all my training to "think good thoughts," "look on the bright side," and "take it a day at a time," I woke up to a near-miserable world. This little boy who knows nothing of optimism woke up, saw he had a new day, and gave it his grandest praise. I learned something.

It dawned on me that this innocent little child was at the place I wanted to be. To wake up in the morning, take a look at the world, and say "wow" is probably about as close to contentment as a person can ever hope to get.

Contentment is a rare commodity. The more we learn about this world, the more anxious we get. There is trouble afoot. There are heartbreaks, failures, tragedies, and an endless list of selfish desires that are never realized. Sooner or later we come to resent our own existence. I'm sure our innocent child will eventually eat this forbidden apple and wake up, as most of us do, to say only "ugh."

I wish I knew what I could do to never let this happen. I wish he could teach me the way he sees things now so that I could help him hold on to it — and so I could remember how it's done. That truly would be a "most important thing" — if this tiniest of guides can show me from his crib how to open my eyes in the morning, see that I am alive in Paradise, and say "wow."

Father's Day

This Father's Day business is kind of new to me. I've only recently become a father, so I'm not sure what to expect, but I like the idea of it. It's sort of like inheriting another birthday at midlife. We become the centers of attention and objects of affection for a whole sweet Sunday. And we get presents. I guess that's what interests me.

It doesn't interest me in a selfish way, really. I'm just curious what type of present a dad like me would get. I don't feel I cut quite the figure of a father that, say, my dad did when I lived in his house. He was big, wore suits, and smelled of cologne and shaving cream. We could get him ties or Old Spice and end up being pretty good kids for the effort.

You couldn't get me a tie. I already have one, and it's in the back of the closet with the knot still in it. I couldn't keep a straight face if you got me Old Spice or a soap-on-a-rope. My dad might have laughed at soap-on-a-rope too, but he would have hung it on the showerhead all the same.

I got him a rock one year with a magazine picture pasted to it. I made it myself. It was meant to be a paperweight, but he could have used it for a doorstop, too. Actually, he could have derailed a train with it. The magazine picture was pretty good-sized, and I had to use a big rock to fit it all on. I think the only reason he kept it around was there was no place he could throw it away.

My son isn't old enough yet to design me paperweights, so he and his mother will probably go for something a little more conventional. But just what is a conventional Father's Day gift these days?

Judging by the sale ads in the newspaper, it seems that everything in a hardware store is a "Great Gift Idea for Dad." I thought that kind of thinking went out of style with soap-on-a-rope. It would be like putting floor mops on sale for Mother's Day. To assume that all the family men in America share a common desire for a set of matching screwdrivers is to be more than a little presumptuous.

Fathers are changing. I think that's why I feel a little funny about all this. Gone are the days when you could stand the old man next to a new barbecue on Father's Day, slap a beer in one hand, a spatula in the other, and tie an I'M THE BOSS apron across his pot gut. A lot of dads would rather have a Cuisinart. I know I would.

It's a risky business for a man to buy a woman a kitchen appliance these days. He's likely to be accused of "forcing roles" or what-not upon her. But give a guy a blender, and stand back. He'll wear the blades off of the thing playing with it. Want shakes? Got shakes. Pâté? Try this liver. He'll have it mastered in no time then sit back grinning like a fool, not realizing he's just done what everybody's been trying to get him to do for twenty years.

It's becoming common knowledge that most of today's fathers do more than spit good and go to work. They are, often as not, up all night with the sick kid, rolling Pampers down the grocery aisles, and maybe a little late for work right alongside the working mothers.

So how about something for the working father? Like a men's diaper bag. I'm not exactly sure what a men's diaper bag would look like, but it would make a nice gift. If it was anything like a game pouch or a saddlebag, I'm sure it would do. There's something about a quilted blue bag lined with a floral print that fails to define a guy's masculinity. You can tell me it's all in my head, but it's not. It's hanging on my shoulder. If one more bonehead tells me he "likes my purse," I'm either going to break somebody's nose or break down and cry. It's hard to decide which with an accessory like that at my side.

So you can see that the realm of great gift ideas for Dad has grown a little beyond the tool and fishing tackle departments. That's not to say those aren't great gifts too, but don't let anybody fool you into thinking that we're not hanging out in kitchens and sizing up car seats with the best of them.

Who knows what sort of Father's Day gifts I'll accumulate over the years. As my son grows up and gets to know me, I'm sure he'll pick out just the right thing. I might not be as easy as Old Spice and a necktie, but I'm pretty easy, and just about anything else would do fine.

I just hope that somewhere among those future Father's Day gifts, whether I get my diaper bag and Cuisinart or not, there's something along the lines of a large rock with a picture pasted to it. There isn't a dad in the world that couldn't use one of those.

Not
Letting Go

My mom just sent me a box full of stuff she cleaned out of the attic. Everything's in it from my high school diploma to my infant feeding schedule. It's a pretty important little bit of history that couldn't mean much to anybody but me and my folks.

The first thing out of the box was a print of Mom and Dad's wedding picture. They had six of them made, one for each of the six kids they knew they were going to have. Mom looks like a young Rita Hayworth in a bridal gown. Dad strikes quite a figure himself with a full head of hair and a naval uniform. He is tall and trim with medals on his chest. They look good together. Like they know what they're doing.

There's a small spiral notebook in the box, a record of the first six months of my life written in my mother's young hand. It's sort of humbling to review. I tasted my first cereal thirty-two years ago this coming May 9. I cut my first tooth the following June 3, a tooth that probably earned me a nickel under my pillow a few years later. I got my first haircut on Tuesday, July 26, and the record leaves off a few days later. On the last page I weigh eighteen pounds, three ounces.

None of us really remembers being a baby, and it's sort of nice to see this evidence that I once was. Under the notebook I found a packet of cards. They're congratulation cards that friends and relatives sent my folks when I was born. None of them mention me by name, so I must not have had one yet. One of them is a florist's card from Peter and Billy. Peter was my father's name before it was Dad. Billy was my older brother, who's now a mechanical engineer in Philadelphia named Bill. One card starts, "Welcome, little darling." It's from a grandmother who died sixteen years ago.

Am I boring you with all this? Probably. Who knows why people save these sorts of things. For just this reason, I suppose. To be able one day to send it off to a grown child and say, "Once you were ours." We forget that, I think. After all, we spend most of our young lives denying it. Something inside tells us to fight our parents every inch of the way until we leave home or get thrown out.

I see it already in our own young son. The rebellious acts of treason. Cries of defiance from a screwed-up little face. Always testing, always stretching the bonds to the breaking point, then returning. No parents can watch their children finding their legs under them without a little sadness. As we nervously monitor their awkward progress step by ill-placed step, we know that one day we'll have to watch grown legs carry them out of our lives.

A contemporary version of the box my mom just sent me is beginning to take shape in our bedroom closet. I never really knew what we were going to do with all that junk until now. Silly records and sentiments that couldn't mean much to much of anybody. They won't amount to a lot compared to the disagreements we're bound to have over the next twenty or thirty years. We'll give them little thought as we suffer through the pratfalls of his becoming a man.

God willing, he will become one. I hope a happy one with a good mind, a safe home, and a family of his own. I hope he's vital, and strong-willed. I hope he's good at what he does, and does good with it. Mostly I hope he'll be able to look one day into a box full of yellowed notebooks and curling photographs and ponder for a minute the fact he once was ours. Then I hope when he's a father he starts putting together a box of his own. There are certain silly things in this world that shouldn't be let go of.

About
the Author

Tom Bodett was born in 1955 and grew up in Sturgis, Michigan. He has been a cannery worker, a logger, an independent building contractor, and a commentator on National Public Radio's "All Things Considered." He is the author of a previous collection, *As Far As You Can Go Without a Passport,* and is the national media pitchman for Motel 6. He lives with his wife and son in Homer, Alaska, from where he hosts "The End of the Road Review," a weekly radio variety show now broadcast on over 100 stations.